THEORIES OF SOCIAL CHANGE

THEORIES OF
SOCIAL CHANGE

RICHARD P. APPELBAUM
University of Chicago

MARKHAM PUBLISHING COMPANY / Chicago

MARKHAM SOCIOLOGY SERIES
Robert W. Hodge, Editor

Adams, *Kinship in an Urban Setting*

Adams, *The American Family: A Sociological Interpretation*

Adams and Weirath, eds., *Readings on the Sociology of the Family*

Appelbaum, *Theories of Social Change*

Farley, *Growth of the Black Population: A Study of Demographic Trends*

Filstead, ed., *Qualitative Methodology: Firsthand Involvement with the Social World*

Karp and Kelly, *Toward an Ecological Analysis of Intermetropolitan Migration*

Laumann, Siegel, and Hodge, eds., *The Logic of Social Hierarchies*

Zeitlin, ed., *American Society, Inc.: Studies of the Social Structure and Political Economy of the United States*

This paper was prepared under predoctoral Research Training Grant S FO1 MH39098–03 BEH

CONTENTS

Introduction

This book reviews theories of social change according to what are felt to be the dominant paradigms in the field. Following Kuhn's (1962:10) usage, by "paradigms" I mean models which give rise to particular coherent traditions of scientific research. Social Sciences, unlike what Kuhn terms the "normal sciences," are seldom characterized by widely accepted paradigms at any given point in time: there is, in fact, little agreement among social scientists regarding the proper categorization of such limited paradigms as may indeed exist or the proper classification of scientists into whatever schema is devised.[1] In the following chapters, a particular categorization of the field of social change is offered, along with an appropriate classification of students of social change. The categories—along with illustrative cases in each—depart somewhat from those employed by other writers. Several alternative classifications of theories of social change are reviewed in Chapter 5, where they are considered in light of the schema presented in the text.

[1] Perhaps "schools" would be a more appropriate term than paradigms, since in Kuhn's treatment of the subject he regards normal science as being guided by a single principal paradigm at any given time.

Before proceeding with the review of theories of social change, it will be necessary to delimit our effort in the interest of manageability; to do so, it will be necessary to narrowly circumscribe what is meant by both "social" and "change."

Preliminary Definitions

For purposes of delimiting an area of concern, it is convenient to distinguish four levels of human action—the individual personality, interactions among individuals, the group or social system, and the cultural system. These levels are chosen in that they correspond roughly to empirical treatments of the "social" in the literature. Various authors (and few consistently) have regarded social action as residing principally in the individual, in the interaction between individuals, as an emergent property of large groups, and in the symbols that characterize human interaction. The first level has historically been the province of psychologists, whether they follow a psychoanalytic or a behaviorist model. For Freud (1958: 215), the nature of the social relations among men—and the sum of those relations that constitutes civilization—is in large part traceable to infant sexuality and instinctive egoism:

> By the admixture of erotic components the egoistic instincts are transmuted into *social* ones. We learn to value being loved as an advantage for which we are willing to sacrifice other advantages. . . . Civilization is the fruit of renunciation of instinctual satisfaction, and from each new-comer in turn it exacts the same renunciation.[2]

[2] While it is true that Freud gave major emphasis to "instinctive" aspects of the personality (id, libido) and their repression in explaining both human psychopathology and the pathologies of society (see Freud, 1961), the individual's nexus of social relations was introduced into the calculus via the concept of the superego. This provides an entree into psychoanalytic theory for sociologists and social psychologists who seek to explain social behavior primarily in terms of interaction among individuals. T. Parsons and R. F. Bales (1955) provide an example of one such marriage between sociology and psychology.

Behavioral psychologists (Proshansky and Seidenberg, 1965: 6) also focus primarily on the individual, attempting to explain the relationships between the properties of the physical world and what they identify as fundamental psychological processes (cognition, emotion, motivation). The emphasis here, at least experimentally, is on the individual's response to externally induced stimuli; insofar as possible, these stimuli are abstracted from the social world, which is either ignored or held *ceterus paribus*. "In the laboratory the effects of social factors are minimized or held constant, and . . . essentially the properties of the basic psychological processes in relation to the physical world are revealed (6)."

The second level constitutes the province of social psychology, in particular, students of group dynamics. It constitutes what has been called the "behaviorist perspective," including personality, interaction, and self theory. Social psychology, at least according to two of its practitioners (Proshansky and Seidenberg 1965: 4), is "first, concerned with the behaving *individual* (including what he experiences), and, second, the context in which this behavior takes place, that is, the *social setting*—other individuals or groups." Georg Simmel (1964: 14–15, italics added) locates the social in the interaction among individuals (rather than in the individual or the group) : "At one time it appeared as if there were only two consistent subject matters of the science of man: the individual unit and the unit of individuals (society) ; any third seemed logically excluded. . . . A more comprehensive classification of the science of the relations of men should distinguish, it would appear, *those relations which constitute a unit,* that is, social relations in the strict sense. . . ." Meadian psychology not only sees the social level as residing in the relations among men, but sees the human personality as arising virtually entirely from human interaction: "The self is something which has a development; it is not initially there at birth but arises in the process of social experience and activity, that is, develops in the given individual as a result of his relations to that process as a whole and to other individuals within that process" (Mead, 1964: 199).

The third level has typically been the concern of sociologists. It focuses on the group as the unit of analysis, and particularly the emergent properties of the group—wherein the social level is felt to reside. Emile Durkheim (1964: 13) set this concern with his definition of "social facts" as "every way of acting, fixed or not, capable of exercising on the individual an external constraint." Exteriority (to the individual) and constraint (on the individual) characterize social action, the province of inquiry unique to sociology.

> Whenever . . . elements combine and thereby produce, by the fact of their combination, new phenomena, it is plain that these new phenomena reside not in the original elements but in the totality formed by their union (Durkheim, 1964: xlvii).
>
> Let us apply this principle to sociology. If, as we may say, this synthesis constituting every society yields new phenomena, differing from those which take place in individual consciousness, we must, indeed, admit that these facts reside exclusively in the very society itself which produces them, and not in its parts, i.e., its members. They are, then, in this sense external to individual consciousness (xlviii). . . . Here, then, are ways of acting, thinking; and feeling that present the noteworthy property of existing outside the individual consciousness.
>
> These types of conduct or thought are not only external to the individual but are, moreover, endowed with coercive power, by virtue of which they impose themselves upon him, independent of his individual will (2).

Much of the concern of 20th century American sociology has been with aspects of social action. Indeed, the analysis of structural effects on behavioral variables—the sociological model for which was set forth by Durkheim himself in his study of suicide in 1897—has been the *sine qua non* of American empirical sociology for half a century. Studies of bureaucracy (Blau, 1960: 178–193), ecology (Robinson, 1950: 351–357), social stratification and social mobility (see Bendix and Lipset, 1966: esp. secs. IV–V)—studies employing measures of context or group characteristics (such as structure) as explanatory variables—would fall into this category. Nor is such emphasis limited to American empirical sociology. Matters of method notwithstanding, Marx's concept of the "social" is certainly compatible with that of Durkheim's, since the former's concept of class consciousness closely parallels the latter's collective conscience, both in nature and in function. For Marx as for Durkheim, man is constrained by the group, both in thought and in action; the group, or class, has an existence above and apart from that of its membership,[3] and individual behavior reflects the exteriority of the group. As defined by Durkheim, a social group may be comprised of a small unit of coworkers, a social class, or a nation-state—provided, of course, that the group has sufficient reality *as a group* to exercise constraint or otherwise affect the individual.

The fourth level has generally been considered the subject matter of anthropology. It is concerned with what Parsons (1966: 5) has termed the cultural component of human action: "human action is 'cultural' in that meanings and intentions concerning acts are formed in terms of *symbolic* systems (including the codes through which they operate in patterns) that focus most generally about the universal of human society, language." While Parsons clearly distinguishes between cultural and social systems, the term "culture" enjoys a usage even less restricted than "social;" most anthropologists appear to include much of what we have previously termed social in their usage of the term culture. Hoebel (1960: 168), for example, defines culture as "the integrated sum total of learned behavior traits which are manifest and shared by the members of a society," while Murdock (1960: 248; see Kroeber and Kluckhohn, 1952, for a systematic treatment of definitions of culture) notes that "a culture consists of habits that are shared by members of a society." Major distinctions in anthropological literature include those between material (technology) and non-material culture, and between culture as a configuration of existential postulates (about the na-

[3] Marx attributed class formation to the tensions between the forces of production and the relations of production that exist at any point in time.

ture of things) and as a configuration of normative postulates[4] (about the desirability of things) (Hoebel, 1960: 116–
117). Steward (1955: 43–97) apparently uses the terms
"culture," "cultural system," and "sociocultural systems"
interchangeably; his definitions correspond to Hoebel's
(1955: see chap. 1). In general, it would appear that culture refers to characteristics of human behavior and their
transmission over time, rather than to human interactions
per se, and that major emphasis is given to the learning
and transmission of values and symbols.

In the analysis which follows in subsequent sections
of this paper, we shall limit ourselves largely to the third
and fourth levels described above. More specifically, we
shall be concerned with theories of societal change and the
social changes which accompany changes at the societal
level. In selecting theories for discussion, we shall follow
Parsons (1966: 2; see also Gould and Kolb, 1964: 674–
675; Sills, 1968: vol. 14, 577–586) in defining society as
"relatively the most self-sufficient type of social system," [5]
although this definition will serve primarily as a guideline,
inasmuch as it will be necessary to work with the definitions
(explicit or implicit) that characterize each theory under
consideration. Cultural change is included primarily because theorists of cultural change generally use the term
generically to include much of what would otherwise be
included under the rubric "social change." Since the two
levels are distinguished by relatively few theorists, we shall
likewise be forced to ignore the distinction in the case of
most theorists; we can only remain sensitive to the distinction, calling attention to it where possible. The justi-
fication for limiting this paper to theories of societal change
is twofold: first, the area so delimited is of principal interest to the writer; and second, considerations of brevity

[4] W. F. Ogburn also emphasized the distinction between material
and nonmaterial culture. See Chapter 2.

[5] David Aberle (1950: 110–111) offers a similar but more complete definition: "A Society is a group of human beings sharing a
self-sufficient system of action which is capable of existing longer
than the life-span of an individual, the group being recruited at least
in part by the sexual reproduction of its members."

make it necessary to delimit the field in some fashion. We will *not* be looking at theories that are exclusively concerned with such things as social movements, group dynamics, organizational change, changes in demographic patterns, or changes in societal subsystems (the polity, the economy, the family, etc.). We will be concerned with theories that raise such matters in the context of their ramifications throughout the social structure. Though such exclusions preclude any possibility of devising an overarching framework for the analysis of all social change, few sociologists have ever attempted an inclusive analysis, and none who have done so have met with great success.[6]

Having completed the discussion of what is "social" in change, it is now necessary to briefly consider what is meant by "change." Various distinctions are useful.

(1) Magnitude of change: large-scale v. small-scale

[6] Smelser (1968) has made a major effort to systematically review and synthesize existing theories of social change. His classification of existing theories is based on two principal dimensions: whether the theories are concerned with disintegrative or reconstructive processes, and whether they are concerned with short-term or long-term processes. He thus takes into account both time horizon and the direction of change. Smelser reviews one theory for each of the four types thus created: theories of social collapse in crisis conditions; theories of long-term decline, decay, or death; theories of recovery from crisis conditions; and theories of long-term development or growth. Additionally, he reviews two theories which incorporate elements of both long-term decline *and* development—Marxism, and some later theoretical works by Bronislaw Malinowski. In synthesizing these approaches into a single unified one, Smelser follows several steps: (1) The organization of variables into different classes of equilibrium systems, including a shock-and-ramifications model; a stable dynamic equilibrium model, a series of unstable equilibrium states model; a stable moving equilibrium model; a series of long-term stable or cyclical equilibrium states superimposed on a long-term moving stable equilibrium model; a series of stable dynamic short-run equilibrium states superimposed on a long-term unstable dynamic equilibrium model; a series of unstable equilibrium states superimposed on a long-term trend towards stable equilibrium model. (2) The specification of sequence or phases of change, including the following: the appearance of some impetus to change; response to this impetus; intermediate phase; and a phase of long-term structural and cultural change. Each phase is further subdivided. Another theorist who gives explicit attention to the interrelationship between changes at different levels is Talcott Parsons; his general theory is intended to cover all human action. See in particular Parsons (1960; 1966).

change. The magnitude of change will reflect a number of characteristics of the units affected [7] the size and centrality (or strategic character) of the units affected; the proportion of affected units in the system; the susceptibility of the affected unit to change (its degree of resistance to change); the degree of alteration involved by the change; and the suddenness of the onset of the impetus to change. The utility of these distinctions is primarily in calling attention to the importance of scale and its possible components.

(2) Time span of change: Long- v. short-term change. The length of the period over which change occurs is clearly an important distinction. Smelser (1968: 269–271) utilizes time horizon as one of two dimensions on which he characterizes all theories of social change as well as one of the key variables in synthesizing these theories into a new, general formulation of processes of change. This distinction appears to underly Ogburn's theory of the cultural lag, although it is not always clear in Ogburn's treatment of lag whether the length of the lag or the degree of maladjustment is critical. The theory of the demographic transition is another instance in which the time horizon of change is formally treated as of major importance; both Ogburn (1964: 86) and Hauser (1969: 1–19) have treated this as an example of lag.

(3) Effect on the changing unit: Process v. structural change. Parsons (1966: 20–21) distinguishes between those processes that serve to maintain a system and those which cause structural changes in it. The former is an equilibrium or homeostasis concept and refers (for Parsons) to the mechanisms by which any system comes to terms with the exigencies imposed by a changing environment (which, of course, can include other systems) without causing an essential change in its own structure. The latter calls attention to system change and (again, for Parsons) is characterized primarily by the process of structural differentiation. The distinction between processes which serve to maintain the structure and processes which do not is a critical distinction made by functionalists and other equilibrium theorists; it is not always made by theorists who

[7] These distinctions are adapted from Smelser (1968: 269–271).

view conflict and change as characterizing all social organization. Marx (1959: 20; see also ch. 3, below), of course, emphasized the ubiquity of conflict and its systematic relation to all social structures: "without conflict no progress: this is the law which civilization has followed to the present day." Dahrendorf (1959) and other conflict theorists echo Marx on the ubiquity of conflict.

In subsequent analyses, all three distinctions, the magnitude of change, the time horizon of change, and the effect on the changing unit, will be employed to systematically characterize the theories reviewed. In most cases, and unless otherwise indicated, we will be reviewing theories of large-scale, long-run change. Whether these distinctions are explicitly made by the theorists or must be inferred from their works is of interest. The third distinction will provide a useful device for distinguishing conflict theories from other theories.

The following chapters employ a typology of theories of social change to clarify some of the assumptions regarding the "social" and "change" contained in these theories.[8] The categories are not mutually exclusive; they emphasize major differences in underlying assumptions and their derivative approaches to social change. Theories can be analyzed under more than one general heading and some will be, depending on which aspect of the theory is being considered. Four broad categories are identified: evolutionary theories, characterized primarily by assumptions of smooth, cumulative change, often in a linear fashion, and always in the direction of increasing complexity and adaptability; equilibrium theory, characterized by the concept of homeostasis, and focusing on conditions tending towards stability as a consequence; conflict theory, characterized by the assumption that change is endemic to all social organisms, and focusing on conditions that tend towards instability as a consequence; and "rise and fall" theories, characterized by the assumption that societies, cultures, or civilizations regress as well as grow—that all societies do not move in the same direction. It is clear that evolutionary theories in some sense

[8] A more extended discussion of this typology is postponed until Chapter 5.

subsume both equilibrium theories and conflict theories; in each of these theories it is assumed that societies can be treated as highly interdependent systems that generally move in the direction of increasing complexity and are concerned with maximizing adaptability to environment. Furthermore, particular variants of both equilibrium and conflict theories share the assumption that change is unilinear, in that all societies move from a similar initial state to a similar final state, both exemplified in the historical experience of the western European nations and the United States. Thus, Parsons' (Parsons and Smelser, 1956: 33–38) early use of pattern-variables identifies a before-and-after set of patterns which characterize pre-industrial and industrial societies (Parsons and Smelser 1965: 33–38),[9] while Marx (Feuer, 1959: 1–41) delineates a specified set of stages all societies must pass through as the class struggle, reflecting the technological organization of production at any given time, runs its course. Why then distinguish evolutionary theories from equilibrium and conflict theories? The distinction is maintained because it calls attention to significant differences in emphasis among the theories: evolutionary theory emphasizes smooth, cumulative change, equilibrium theory emphasizes adjustment and homeostasis among parts, and conflict theory emphasizes inherent instability and change. Depending on which aspect of any particular theory is felt to characterize it or dominate its presentation in any given instance, that theory will be assigned to the appropriate category.

The schema is as follows:

1. EVOLUTIONARY THEORY

    A. Classical Evolutionary Theory: Notions of Progress
       i. Darwin
      ii. Unilinear theories of social progress

---

[9] Four of the dichotomies were borrowed from Toennies' Gemeinschaft-Gesellschaft distinction: self v. collectivity orientation, universalism v. particularism, functional-specificity v. functional diffuseness, and affectivity v. affective neutrality. The fifth, adapted from Linton, is the distinction between ascription and achievement.

REFERENCES

Aberle, David.
  1950 "The functional prerequisites of society." Ethics
     60: 100–11.

Bendix, Reinhard, and Seymour M. Lipset, eds.
  1966   Class, Status, and Power: A Reader in Social
         Stratification. New York: Free Press.
Blau, Peter M.
  1960   "Structural effects." American Sociological Re-
         view 25: 179–93.
Dahrendorf, Ralf.
  1959   Class and Class Conflict in Industrial Society.
         Stanford, Calif.: Stanford University Press.
Durkheim, Emile.
  1964   The Rules of Sociological Method. New York: Free
         Press.
Feuer, Lewis S., ed.
  1959   Marx and Engels: Basic Writings on Politics and
         Philosophy. New York: Doubleday.
Freud, Sigmund.
  1958   On Creativity and the Unconscious. New York:
         Harper & Brothers.
  1961   Civilization and Its Discontents. New York: W.
         W. Norton.
Gould, Julius, and William L. Kolb.
  1964   A Dictionary of the Social Sciences. New York:
         Free Press.
Hauser, Philip M.
  1969   "The chaotic society: Product of the social mor-
         phological revolution." American Sociological Re-
         view 34 (February): 1–19.
Hoebel, E. Adamson.
  1960   "The nature of culture." In Harry L. Shapiro
         (ed.), Man, Culture, and Society. New York: Ox-
         ford University Press.
Kroeber, Alfred L., and Clyde Kluckhohn.
  1952   "Culture: A critical review of concepts and defini-
         tions." Papers of the Peabody Museum of Ameri-
         can Archaeology and Ethnology 47: 1. Cambridge,
         Mass: The Museum.
Kuhn, Thomas S.
  1962   The Structure of Scientific Revolutions. Chicago:
         University of Chicago Press.

Marx, Karl.
  1959 Das Elend der Philosophie. As quoted and trans-
         lated in Ralf Dahrendorf, Class and Class Conflict
         in Industrial Society. Stanford, Calif.: Stanford
         University Press.
Mead, George Herbert.
  1964 On Social Psychology. Chicago: University of Chi-
         cago Press.
Moore, Wilbert E.
  1963 Social Change. Englewood Cliffs, N.J.: Prentice-
         Hall.
Murdock, George Peter.
  1960 "How culture changes." In Harry L. Shapiro (ed.),
         Man, Culture, and Society. New York: Oxford
         University Press.
Ogburn, William F.
  1964 On Culture and Social Change. Chicago: University
         of Chicago Press.
Parsons, Talcott.
  1960 Structure and Process in Modern Societies. New
         York: Free Press.
  1966 Societies: Evolutionary and Comparative Per-
         spectives. Englewood Cliffs, N.J.: Prentice-Hall.
Parsons, Talcott, and Robert F. Bales.
  1955 Family, Socialization, and Interaction Process.
         New York: Free Press.
Parsons, Talcott, and Neil J. Smelser.
  1956 Economy and Society. New York: Free Press.
Proshansky, Harold, and Bernard Seidenberg.
  1965 Basic Studies in Social Psychology. New York:
         Holt, Rinehart & Winston.
Robinson, William S.
  1950 "Ecological correlations and the behavior of in-
         dividuals." American Sociological Review 15: 351–
         57.
Shapiro, Harry L., ed.
  1960 Man, Culture, and Society. New York: Oxford
         University Press.

Sills, David L., ed.
   1968   International Encyclopedia of the Social Sciences.
          Vol. 14. New York: Macmillan; Free Press.
Simmel, Georg.
   1964   Conflict and the Web of Group Affiliations. New
          York: Free Press.
Smelser, Neil J.
   1968   Essays in Sociological Explanation. Englewood
          Cliffs, N.J.: Prentice-Hall.
Steward, Julian H.
   1955   Theory of Culture Change. Urbana: University
          of Illinois Press.

1
Evolutionary Theory

19th century evolutionary theories were characterized by implicit or explicit notions of progress. Strongly influenced by Darwin's work in biological evolution, theorists often sought a sociological analogue to the living organism. Although the earlier theories were highly evaluative in defining progress in terms of western industrial society, Spencer and Durkheim developed a model of organismic evolution that has strongly influenced sociological thinking to the present day. Twentieth century theories of "modernization," such as the industrialization of African, Asian, and Latin American nations, are the direct legacy of the earlier evolutionary theories, although the influence of the earlier theories is also clearly present in functionalist and systems theory. Recently, evolutionary theories have been revitalized in neoevolutionary theories that build on the anthropological and sociological evidence of the 20th century, and thus avoid some of the bias and pitfalls that discredited their 19th century predecessors.

CLASSICAL EVOLUTIONARY THEORY: NOTIONS OF PROGRESS

Charles Darwin

Darwin (1887) borrowed heavily from the social sciences. From Malthus, he was struck by the notion of survival of the most fit variations in the universal struggle for existence,[1] and in *The Origin of Species* (1859) he cites Spencer as one of his predecessors. Insofar as it is relevant for the subsequent development of sociology, Darwinian evolution (1859; 1880) is reducible to a few key propositions: (1) Tremendous variability exists among species. (2) The population of any given species tends to increase beyond its means of subsistence. (3) As a result, there is a struggle for existence within and among species. (4) In this struggle, the strongest or most fit—the best adapted—survive in the long run; the weaker perish. This is the "rigid law of natural selection," (1880: 48) resulting in the survival of the fittest. Darwin was quite explicit about the source of variations among species: he rejected the Lamarckian notion that acquired traits can be inherited, preferring to conceive of variations as arising by chance (mutation).[2] Natural selection, then, assured the survival of those *chance* variations which were most fit: "beneficial variations of all kinds will thus, either occasionally or habitually, have been preserved, and injurious ones eliminated" (48). Thus, for Darwin, there is no question of species adapting themselves to environment; rather, great variety exists and is constantly being introduced, and the variants that are adapted best survive while the others perish. As Stebbins (1967: 225–226) puts it,

> . . . an impression of progressive advancement toward a particular goal can be gained only if we start with a type which we consider advanced,

[1] For example, Malthus discusses the importance of preventive checks such as disease and famine in maintaining the population in balance with its environment.

[2] Support for Darwin's concept of essentially random variation among species occurred with deVries' discovery of mutation in 1900.

such as man, and reconstruct for it a family tree of the particular ancestors of that group, disregarding the immensely greater number of collaterals which never evolved to a state regarded by us as advanced, even though their descendents survive to the present time.

Looking at insects, for example, one notes movement in the direction of both greater complexity and greater simplicity. Ants and bees have evolved in the direction of greater complexity to an extent perhaps greater than man, while fleas and aphids have evolved in the direction of greater simplicity than their ancestors. There is clearly no room for notions of progress in the study of the evolution of organisms unless one defines progress in anthropomorphic terms (Simpson, 1949) or in terms of increased dominance over living and nonliving environment (Huxley, 1942), two definitions which place man in the most highly evolved position. Most variants of evolutionary theory in the social sciences accept one of these two types of definitions of progress—generally the former. Thus, all unilinear theories of progress (Comte, Spencer, social Darwinists), all modernization theories, and all systems theories regard the western industrial, urbanized society (highly complex, specialized, differentiated, and interrelated) as in some sense the end product of evolution. Marx also falls into this category, although he looked beyond current industrial social organization to see a somewhat different end product. The latter definition of progress, dominance over environment, characterizes equilibrium theories, particularly the school of human ecology, and to an extent systems theories, at least insofar as they stress "adaptive upgrading" (Parsons, 1966: 22), in terms of dominance over environment, a notion which generally goes hand-in-hand with overall assumptions of increasing complexity as mentioned above.

Unilinear Theories of Social Progress

If Darwin was influenced by social scientists such as Malthus and Spencer, social science was strongly influenced by Darwin; notions of evolution have dominated social change theory in one form or another since the 19th century. Many early evolutionists were content to merely describe the progress of society from early, "primitive" forms to "advanced" (generally western European) civilization; some, concerned lest the march of civilization impede the process of survival of the fittest through *natural* selection, constructed an elaborate sociological apology for the laissez-faire economics of the "robber barons" that characterized the rapid expansion of capitalism around the turn of the century. This latter group became known as social Darwinists.

Comte, Maine, and Morgan exemplify early attempts to trace the evolution of specific social forms or entire societies from some earlier, less advanced state to a terminal, advanced state—an approach Sahlins (Sahlins and Service, 1960: 12–44) has termed General Evolution.[3] Aspects of Toennies and Spencer also fall into this category. Comte (1964), writing in the early 19th century, applied his positivist method to the study of civilization and came up with a uniform sequence of stages which all cultures, at all times, experience.

> I believe that history may be divided into three grand epochs, or states of civilization, each possessing a distinct character, spiritual and temporal. They embrace civilization at once in its elements and in its *ensemble*. . . .
> Of these the first is the Theological and Military epoch.
> In this state of society, all theoretical conceptions, whether general or special, bear a supernatural impress. The imagination completely dominates over the observing faculty, to which all right of inquiry is denied.
>
> .   .   .
>
> The second epoch is the Metaphysical and Juridical. Its general character is that of pos-

[3] Sahlins (Sahlins and Service, 1960: 12–44) distinguishes General Evolution—the emergence of "higher forms" in terms of dominance over environment—and Specific Evolution, giving rise to cultural diversity. The concept of General Evolution parallels Huxley's notion of evolutionary progress. We shall return to Sahlins in the discussion of neoevolutionary theories later in this chapter.

sesing no well-defined characteristics. It forms a link and is mongrel and transitional.

.   .   .

Lastly, the third epoch is that of Science and Industry. All special theoretical conceptions have become positive, and the general conceptions tend to become so. As regards the former, observation predominates over imagination; while, in reference to the latter, observation has dethroned the imagination, without yet taking its place (19–20).

Much of Comte's work lies in tracing the ramifications of this process in the various social, cultural, and scientific spheres. Comte (18) felt that the progress of civilization followed a natural law resulting "from the instinctive tendency of the human race to perfect itself;" it was thus inevitable and unalterable, and "none of the intermediate steps which it prescribes can be evaded, and no step in a backward direction can really be made" (18).

What then are the modifications of which the social organism and social life are susceptible, if nothing can alter the laws either of harmony or of succession? The answer is that modifications act upon the intensity and secondary operation of phenomena, but without affecting their nature or their filiation . . . the progress of the race must be considered susceptible of modification only with regard to any interval of any importance being overleaped (1893: 76).

Since the state of social organization follows the state of civilization, the same law applies to social organization, indeed, to all civilization "considered as a whole or in its elements" (1964: 18). While Comte claimed to be largely unconcerned with questions of progress or human perfectability, he clearly felt that the long-run movement was in the direction of ever-increasing amelioration, in terms of man's control over his environment as well as the development of his intellectual and moral faculties:

Taking the human race as a whole, and not any one people, it appears that human development brings after it, in two ways, an ever-growing amelioration, first, in the radical condition of Man, which no one disputes; and next, in his corresponding faculties, which is a view much less attended to. There is no need to dwell upon the improvement in the conditions of human existence, both by the increasing action of Man on his environment through the advancement of the sciences and arts, and by the constant amelioration of his customs and manners; and again, by the gradual improvement in social organization. . . .

As for the other aspect of the question, the gradual and slow improvement of human nature, within narrow limits, it seems to me impossible to reject altogether the principle proposed (with great exaggeration, however) by Lamarck, of the necessary influence of a homogeneous and continuous exercise in producing, in every animal organism, and especially in Man, an organic improvement, susceptible of being established in the race, after a sufficient persistence. If we take the best marked case,—that of intellectual development, it seems to be unquestionable that there is a superior aptitude for mental combinations, independent of all culture, among highly civilized people or what comes to the same thing, an inferior aptitude among nations that are less advanced,— the average intellect of the members of those societies being taken for observation. . . . In regard to morals, particularly, I think it indisputable that the gradual development of humanity favours a growing preponderance of the noblest tendencies of our nature (1893: 73–74). . . .

If Comte saw the development of civilization as evolutionary in the sense of uniform progress toward human perfection, he also saw it as evolutionary in the sense of smooth, continuous change; the laws of social change were seen as merely a "form of the great principle, which of the two great constituent elements of Positive Sociology—Order and Progress—makes the second the result and consequence of the first, according to the maxim:—*Progress is the development of Order*" (1875: 152). In accordance with this principle, Comte (1) divided sociology into two concerns, statics and dynamics: "The one, the statical, will treat of the structural nature of this, the chief of organisms; the other, the dynamical, will treat the laws of its actual development."

Comte regarded society as roughly analogous to the biological organism, an analogy which has proven to be of exceeding durability among those sociologists we have classified as evolutionary or equilibrium theorists. "We have thus established a true correspondence between the Statical Analysis of the Social Organism in Sociology, and that of the Individual Organism in Biology" (239). Although Comte (242) warns against pushing the analogy to fanciful limits, he does manage to find some striking parallels when he notes that the living organism is anatomically decomposed into elements, tissues, and organs, while "the Social Organism [is] definitely composed of the Families which are the true elements or cells, next of the Classes or Castes which are its proper tissues, and lastly of the Cities and Communes which are its real organs." In his organismic analogy, Comte (242) directly anticipated Spencer and Durkheim; in distinguishing the functional interdependence of the social organism from the unity that attaches to similarities, he anticipated Durkheim's distinction between mechanical and organic solidarity:

> . . . without separation of function, there would be no true association between a number of families; they would only form an agglomeration, even in a settled community. Distribution of function is the point which marks off the political society, the basis of which is Cooperation [organic solidarity], from the domestic union, the basis of which is sympathy [mechanical solidarity].[4]

Comte was, therefore, close to Durkheim in his vision of long-run evolution in the direction of increasing societal complexity, interdependence, and hence central authority.[5]

[4] For a discussion of Durkheim and Spencer, see the following section in this chapter.

[5] Durkheim saw a steadily increasing number of restitutive laws (and, with them, agencies of regulation); he strongly criticized Spencer for his laissez-faire attitude towards government and his failure to recognize the noncontractual—i.e., public—elements of supposedly private contracts between individuals.

A strong government is essential in the last (industrial) stage of development:

> On the other hand, the noble part played by this Distribution of Functions would be abortive, unless it were completed by a Combination of Efforts, either spontaneous or disciplined. Nay, the division of occupation is very apt to give rise to serious struggles, intensifying as it does differences in habit, opinion, and propensity, between different families. The desire for Cooperation, which cannot be separated from the desire for Independence, must also be regularly satisfied; it finds satisfaction in that primary social institution, founded to secure joint action. A power to amalgamate men is the more needed that the combative and self-regarding instincts are more energetic than those which prompt us to union. This is the part of that cohesive force in society, everywhere called *government*, the business of which is at once to combine and to direct (243).
> This last condition of Order, a Governing Power, springs spontaneously out of the inequalities between men, upon the separation of social functions (244).

Thus, as society—the Great Being—develops in the direction of ever-increasing functional specialization, it becomes necessary for a strong central authority to provide the requisite coordination among specialized groups which are totally incapable in all areas save their individual specialties.[6] Comte worked out the organization of the new society in elaborate detail, including its domestic life (of which women were seen as the moral guardians), its government (composed of the industrial elite), and its new religion of humanity (in which Comte envisioned himself high priest). The criticisms of Comte (see, for example, Durkheim, 1964: chap. 2), particularly methodological, are numerous and need not be repeated here. From an evolutionary perspective, however, it must be noted that Comte focused on the

[6] Marx saw conflict as arising from vertical differentiation into classes; Comte saw instability as arising from excessive horizontal differentiation into specialized groups.

inner logic of evolution—i.e., the notion that any given culture is driven by an inner mechanism (man's instinctive tendency to perfect himself) through a fixed sequence of stages, despite its unique ecological situation or intercourse with other cultures. Each civilization individually replicates the pattern followed by all civilizations; identity, not diversity, characterizes cultural change. In asserting that evolution is unilineal and individually experienced by each culture, Comte anticipated other theories of evolution, such as those reviewed immediately below. In analyzing the development and consequences of functional differentiation, he paved the way for Spencer and, particularly, for Durkheim.

Henry Sumner Maine (1907) traced the unilineal development of societal progress from relationships based on status to relationships based on contract. Examining the development of Roman law, Maine concluded that ancient societies were based on patriarchal relationships (they were organized around the eldest male in each household, whose dominion over all household members was absolute). The individual's position in society and his opportunities in life were ascribed according to his family status. The ancient concept of power was undifferentiated; the ancient term for power covered all forms of power, as the patriarch had absolute authority:

> Patriarchal Power of all sorts appears, for instance, to have been once conceived as identical in character, and it was doubtless distinguished by one name. The Power exercised by the ancestor was the same whether it was exercised over the family or the material property—over flocks, herds, slaves, children, or wife. We cannot be absolutely certain of its old Roman name, but there is very strong reason for believing, from the number of expressions indicating shades of the notion of power into which the word *manus* enters, that the ancient general term was *manus*. But, when Roman law has advanced a little, both the name and the idea have become specialised. Power is discriminated, both in word and conception, according to the object over which it is exerted (330).

Under the impact of the Roman army and civil administration, however, the state came to replace the family as the principal object of loyalty, and individuals came to realize increasing freedom. The power of the patriarch was supplanted by that of the individual.

> Nor is it difficult to see what is the tie between man and which replaces by degrees those forms of reciprocity in rights and duties which have their origin in the Family. It is Contract. Starting, as from one terminus of history, from a condition of society in which all the relations of Persons are summed up in the relations of Family, we seem to have steadily moved towards a phase of social order in which all these relations arise from the free agreement of Individuals (172–174).

Thus, the status of slave was replaced by the contractual relationship of servant to master. The same progression characterizes other relationships—such as the association between unmarried females and their guardians and adult sons and their fathers.

> All the forms of Status . . . were derived from, and to some extent are still coloured by, the powers and privileges anciently residing in the family . . . we may say that the movement of the progressive societies has hitherto been a movement *from Status to Contract* (174).

Maine (349) traced the development from status to contract in Roman Law from the original *Nexum*, in which the transaction between two parties was fully consummated at the time of the actual exchange, "and in which the formalities which accompany the agreement are even more important than the agreement itself," through several intermediate stages (Stipulation, Literal Contract, Real Contract), to the final stage—the Consensual Contract. In this last stage, the actual exchange need not take place at the time of the transaction, but need only be agreed to by both parties. In determining whether or not the contract is binding, "the mental attitude of the contractors is solely regarded" (349). Maine felt that the Roman law had had an enormous impact on the historical development of many areas outside the field of jurisprudence; "I know of nothing more wonderful than the variety of sciences to which Roman law, Roman contract law more particularly, has contributed modes of thought, courses of reasoning, and a technical language (350–351)." His conception of the evolution from status relationships to contract relationships has influenced subsequent sociological theory; Linton's (1936) distinction between ascribed and achieved statuses, which has reached the sociological literature by way of Parsons and Levy, is an example.

Also important is Maine's treatment of functional differentiation in which he recognizes that institutions (such as the Law) undergo progressive functional specialization, reflected in a concomitant specialization in the conceptions and terminology that relate to them: "an ancient legal conception corresponds not to one but to several modern conceptions. An ancient technical expression serves to indicate a variety of things which in modern law have separate names allotted to them" (Maine, 1907: 329–330). Contemporary evolutionary theorists (for example, Parsons, 1951; 1960: Part 2) have described the process of functional differentiation in similar terms. It should also be noted that in employing polar types—an origin and a destination, describing a continuum which all societies must traverse— Maine anticipated the modernization theorists as well as aspects of the writings of many other sociologists.[7]

Lewis Henry Morgan, writing around the same time as Maine, saw societies as moving through a fixed series of stages as they progressed "from Savagery through Barbarism to Civilization."

> As it is undeniable that portions of the human family have existed in a state of savagery, other portions in a state of barbarism, and still other portions in a state of civilization, it seems equally so that these three distinct conditions are connected with each other in a natural as well as

[7] Parsons (1951), in his pattern variables, Linton, and Toennies are prominent examples.

necessary sequence of progress. Moreover, that this sequence has been historically true of the entire human family, up to the status attained by each branch respectively, is rendered probable by the conditions under which all progress occurs (3). . . .

The development of technology, government, kinship, property, and other institutions is traced through the several stages and their substages, in order "to present some evidence of human progress" (6) on the basis of historical and anthropological evidence. Even architecture provides support for the thesis of man's progress:

House architecture, which connects itself with the form of the family and the plan of domestic life, affords a tolerably complete illustration of progress from savagery to civilization. Its growth can be traced from the hut of the savage, through the communal houses of the barbarians, to the house of the single family of civilized nations, with all the successive links by which one extreme is connected with the other (5).

The state of subsistence technology provides the basis for the classification by ethnical periods, which are summarized by Morgan (12) as follows:

I. Lower Status of Savagery,
        From the Infancy of the Human
        Race to the commencement of
        the next Period.
II. Middle Status of Savagery,
        From the acquisition of a fish
        subsistence and a knowledge of
        the use of fire, to etc.
III. Upper Status of Savagery,
        From the Invention of the Bow
        and Arrow, to etc.
IV. Lower Status of Barbarism,
        From the Invention of the Art
        of Pottery, to etc.
V. Middle Status of Barbarism,
        From the Domestication of an-
        imals on the Eastern hemi-

sphere, and in the Western from
the cultivation of maize and
plants by Irrigation, with the
use of adobe-brick and stone, to
etc.
VI. Upper Status of Barbarism,
From the Invention of the process of smelting Iron Ore, with
the use of iron tools, to etc.
VII. Status of Civilization,
From the Invention of a Pho-
netic Alphabet, with the use of
writing, to the present time.

Morgan's theory was descriptive rather than explanatory, and on the descriptive level it was found to be seriously
wanting: subsequent empirical research indicated that
many societies do not fit into Morgan's stages, that societies
borrow from other societies as well as develop from within,
and that some of Morgan's examples were inaccurately por-
trayed. Institutions simply did not hang together at the
various stages as Morgan had claimed. A most serious
criticism of Morgan's work, however, is that it shares with
other evolutionary theories the notion that progress is defined by the current state of western European civilization:
thus, as suggested by the subtitle to *Ancient Society,*
Morgan's theory was value-laden and far from precise.

Ferdinand Toennies (1964: 64–72) set up two ideal
polar types ("normal concepts") of social organization.
The defining characteristic of each type was held to be the
dominant form of "human willing" which determined the
nature of social relationships. Thus, there are two forms of
human will, rational will (*Kurwille*) and natural will
(*Wesenwille*), and the two forms of social organization, the
Gesellschaft and the *Gemeinschaft,* correspond to these. The
Gemeinschaft, which characterized rural or folklife, was
rapidly being replaced by the cosmopolitan, rational *Gesellschaft* of urban life.

To conclude our theory, two periods stand thus
contrasted with each other in the history of the
great systems of culture: a period of *Gesellschaft*
follows a period of *Gemeinschaft.* The *Gemein-*

schaft is characterized by the social will as concord, folkways, mores, and religion; the *Gesellschaft* by the social will as convention, legislation,
and public opinion. The concepts correspond to
types of external social organization, which may
be classed as follows:

A. *Gemeinschaft*

1. Family life: concord. Man participates in this
   with all his sentiments. Its real controlling
   agent is the people (*Volk*).
2. Rural village life: folkways and mores. Into
   this, man enters with all his mind and heart.
   Its real controlling agent is the commonwealth.
3. Town life: religion. In this, the human being
   takes part with his entire conscience. Its real
   controlling agent is the church.

B. *Gesellschaft*

1. City life: convention. This is determined by
   man's intentions. Its real controlling agent is
   Gesellschaft per se.
2. National life: legislation. This is determined
   by man's calculations. Its real controlling agent
   is the state.
3. Cosmopolitan life: public opinion. This is
   evolved by man's consciousness. Its real controlling agent is the republic of scholars.

With each of these categories a predominant oc-
cupation and a dominating tendency in intellectual life are related in the following manner:

(A) 1. Home (or household) economy, based
       upon liking or preference, *viz.*, the joy
       and delight of creating and conserving.
       Understanding develops the norms for
       such an economy.
    2. Agriculture, based upon habits, *i.e.*, reg-
       ularly repeated tasks. Cooperation is
       guided by custom.
    3. Art, based upon memories, *i.e.*, of in-
       struction, or rules followed, and of ideas
       conceived in one's own mind. Belief in
       the work and the task unites the artistic
       wills.

(B) 1. Trade based upon deliberation; namely, attention, comparison, calculation are the basis of all business. Commerce is deliberate action per se. Contracts are the custom and creed of business.
   2. Industry based upon decision; namely, of intelligent productive use of capital and sale of labor. Regulations rule the factory.
   3. Science, based upon concepts, as is self-evident. Its truths and opinions then pass into literature and the press and thus become part of public opinion (71–72).

Toennies (70–71) viewed this development with some alarm, for

City life and *Gesellschaft* drive the common people to decay and death; in vain they struggle to attain power through their own multitude, and it seems to them that they can use their power only for a revolution if they want to free themselves from their fate . . . The entire culture has been transformed into a civilization of state and *Gesellschaft,* and this transformation means the doom of culture itself if none of its scattered seeds remain alive and again bring forth the essence and idea of *Gemeinschaft,* thus secretly fostering a new culture amidst the decaying one.

Toennies' thought represented a synthesis of his reading of many earlier writers, including Marx, Hobbes, Maine and Wundt (see Martindale, 1960); in turn, he was to have a notable influence on American sociology, particularly through the works of Parsons (Parsons and Smelser, 1956: 34) who, in his early works, adapted several of Toennies dichotomous variables to his own pattern variables.[8] It must be remembered, however, that Toennies was describing ideal types of social organization; although he believed that, historically, one type had replaced the other, he attributed no notions of progress to this movement, but expressed concern with the future and even some horror. Toennies did

---

[8] The four pattern variables are listed in footnote 9 of the Introduction.

not feel that the *Gemeinschaft* was necessarily doomed to extinction. He did fear the possibility but expressed the hope that it would survive through the development of new institutions, *gemeinschaftliche* in nature but adapted to the modern urban culture.

Organismic Theories: Specialization, Differentiation, and Integration

Two sociologists who have had significant impact on contemporary sociological theory, Spencer and Durkheim, wrote within the evolutionary tradition of the late 19th century. They are classified as evolutionists not because they set forth unilinear theories of progress (Durkheim would explicitly have rejected such a position), but because their theories are mainly theories of ever-increasing societal complexity and interrelatedness. Thus, their positions are closer to the biological concepts of evolution than are the sociologists previously discussed, for they focus attention on adaptation through specialization and see societies as highly complex organisms with many specialized and integrated parts, caught up in a process of differentiation and reintegration. The analogy to biological models is, of course, imperfect, for the concept of chance or random variation, and hence survival of the most well adapted (chance) variants, is not present in the sociological formulations. Apparently, there is no social analogy to genetic mutation.

Herbert Spencer developed the analogy between society and living organisms. Both grow throughout their life cycle, increase in mass or size and, at the same time, increase in structure from a few like parts to numerous interrelated unlike parts. Evolution is regarded as a process whereby "matter passes from an indefinite, incoherent homogeneity to a definite, coherent heterogeneity" (Spencer, 1958: 394). A great increase in complexity thus attends growth. At first, even the role of chief is not clearly differentiated; the members of primitive societies "are subject to no control but such as is temporarily acquired by the stronger, or more cunning, or more experienced; not even a permanent nucleus is present" (1892; 1964: 22–24). The first social differentiation, then, occurs in a society that is composed of a hundred or more individuals; this differentiation is that of government or (in its rudimentary form) chieftainship. The next differentiation is between regulative and operative parts and corresponds to the distinction between external and internal conditions. Men, for example, carry on external or regulative activities (primarily warfare with other societies), and women perform the operative tasks associated with subsistence. The structure becomes more complicated as the society increases in number. Functions associated with sustenance, distribution, and regulation become the province of increasingly specialized structures. Power is distributed among numerous chieftains, all under a chief. Differentiation is thus associated with "still greater complexity in the governing agency, with its king, local rulers, and petty chiefs; and, at the same time, there arise more marked divisions of classes—military, priestly, slave, etc. Clearly, then, complication of structure accompanies increase of mass" (12). Large-scale societies evolve, covering widespread areas of varying geographical and ecological character; the parts become dissimilar as they become increasingly specialized. Through trade, the parts of such societies become interdependent, "the like parts being permanently held together [through the chief], mutual dependence becomes possible; and, along with growing mutual dependence, the parts grow unlike. . . ." (12–13). Structural differentiation implies functional differentiation, until many highly specialized skills are being performed by different units of the society. The complex society is thus highly interdependent, and, like the highly developed (e.g., mammalian) organism, cannot survive if central parts are mutilated:

> Let a division be made between the coal mining populations and the adjacent populations which smelt metals or make broadcloth by machinery, and both, forthwith dying socially by arrest of their actions, would begin to die individually. . . .
> In low aggregates, both individual and social, the actions of the parts are but little dependent on one another, whereas in developed aggregates of

> both kinds, that combination of actions which
> constitutes the life of the whole makes possible
> the component actions which constitute the lives
> of the parts (14).

Similarly, society's institutions—analogous to the organs of
the social organism—undergo a parallel development towards coherent heterogeneity. In these terms, Spencer
traces the evolution of the six types of institutions—domestic, ceremonial, political, ecclesiastical, professional, and
industrial.

Spencer was cautious when describing stages or phases
in societal development. He observed that societies tend to
increase in complexity as they increase in mass, but was
reluctant to abstract other general patterns for all societies.
Thus, Spencer felt that industrial societies characterized
by non-coercive regulating systems tend to become dominant,[9] but that industrial societies might become militant
and force the replacement of free, noncoercive, essentially
voluntary institutions with centralized, hierarchical, dis-
ciplined, involuntary systems. Any given type of society will
develop in the direction of increasing complexity; if it re-
sists the necessary changes, it will revert to an earlier state.
In making these conclusions, Spencer, who otherwise shares
the organismic analogy with Comte, emerges as relatively
free of the metaphysical assumptions concerning the in-
evitability of "progress" that characterized the thought of
Comte and some of the earlier evolutionists.

The Division of Labor in Society, written by Emile
Durkheim in 1893 (1964), reformulated many of Spencer's
concepts, but with an emphasis that at the same time defined a subject matter and a methodology for sociology.
Social facts, those aspects of group life which exercise constraint on the individual, are the subject of sociology. The
division of labor is such a fact. In this work, Durkheim
concerned himself with social solidarity as the essential
property of society and developed a methodology of causal
resolution: identify the social facts (e.g., the division of

---

[9] Spencer identified two basic types of societies: industrial societies, in which the internal system dominates, and military societies,
in which the external system dominates.

labor) and establish, first, the efficient cause (e.g., increasing moral density) and, finally, its function (the social need it fulfills: e.g., integration). Durkheim is thus said to be the father of modern functionalism.

Durkheim followed Comte and Spencer in noting that the division of labor produced solidarity in society (its "function," in Durkheim's terms). Unlike Comte and Spencer, however, he sought to identify other sources of solidarity, spell out their relationship over time to the solidarity produced through a division of labor, and attempt to explain this relationship. To do so, Durkheim had to identify social facts which could be used as indicators of different types of solidarity. Following Maine and Toennies, he employed the law as just such an indicator. Several classes of law, each indicative of corresponding classes of solidarity, were identified and their relative weight was assessed. For Durkheim, there were two principal types of solidarity: mechanical solidarity, arising from similarities among individuals, and organic solidarity, arising from the necessary interrelatedness of many unlike but mutually interdependent individuals. Mechanical solidarity is characterized by the existence of a strong collective conscience—that is, states of conscience which are common to all members of society. Its index is penal or criminal law, by which outrages to the collective conscience are avenged. Organic solidarity is characterized by numerous contractual relationships among individuals, and its index is the restitutive (as opposed to expiatory or penal) law, which merely requires restitution to the *status quo ante* and demands no physical penalty. Organic solidarity, then, presupposes great differences and few shared beliefs among individuals—the reverse of mechanical solidarity. Durkheim disagreed with Spencer's conclusion that organic solidarity occurs as a result of an unwritten social contract and effects a diminution of positive controls over the individual in highly complex industrial societies. He reasoned that the laws specifying positive relations (contracts) among individuals were growing in proportion to the replacement of mechanical ties among individuals by organic ties. Contracts, therefore, have an important noncontractual element in that they are invested with a public interest. In fact, Spencer to the contrary, an increasing number of relationships have become imbued with a collective significance and, hence, subject to regulation. Contracts are social (public), not private, affairs.

What, then, is the dynamic of social change for Durkheim? Following Spencer, Durkheim holds that increasing moral density—the number of people in interaction with one another—is critical in determining the nature of social relationships. Initially, societies are small and, correspondingly, the number of persons in potential interaction is small.[10] As moral density increases, societies are segmented into similar units which combine to form larger (but still similar) units. Such primitive, segmented societies are characterized by strong mechanical solidarity: all members share common values, common outlooks, common interpretations, common dialects, and common ways of constructing reality. Punishment is expiatory and violent. Transgression of the law indicates a rejection of widely shared beliefs, and the punishment of such transgressions is essential if the boundaries of correct behavior are to be reaffirmed. Eventually, as the society continues to grow in density, mechanical solidarity ceases to suffice as the sole integrating mechanism. People cease to be similar. While the increased interaction which accompanies increase in population would appear to militate for increased mechanical solidarity, this is true only to a point: thereafter, solidarity breaks down as ideas common to increasing numbers of people become more and more abstract and the possibility for unseen (and hence unpunished) deviance results in a breakdown of norms. Furthermore, resources become scarce, and a division of labor becomes necessary to efficiently exploit scarce resources. Organic solidarity—as indicated by the volume of restitutive law—comes to replace mechanical solidarity in ever-widening areas of life. "The division of labor varies in direct ratio with the volume and density of societies, and, if it progresses in a continuous manner in the course of social development, it is because societies be-

[10] For n people, the number of possible pair interactions is given by $n(n-1)/2$—a measure of social density. See Moore (1963: 55).

come regularly denser and generally more voluminous (Durkheim, 1964: 262).

Is organic solidarity sufficient in itself to integrate a society? Durkheim felt it was not and, in his analysis, was able to identify points of societal stress and to predict their probable rectification in the future. For example, the division of labor, and organic solidarity, presupposes the increasing individuation of man; the cooperative (organic) society develops in the measure that individual personality becomes stronger. Yet the radical individualism Durkheim seems to be pointing to, the nation of highly differentiated units linked together only by their common enterprise and the restitutive laws which regulate the enterprise, is reflected in a tangle of social pathologies. All the old forms of social organization—the family, the community, even the territorial unit—are swept away and replaced by the State, "intrusive as it is impotent" (1951: 389). Lacking a larger collectivity with which he can identify, man lapses into a state of anomie or one of extreme egoism. Both of these stages are reflected in increasing suicide rates. What is the remedy in modern society? The answer, for Durkheim, grew out of his formulation of the problem. Since the differentiation of society occurs along occupational lines, so must the basis for a resurgence of mechanical solidarity, the only form of solidarity which can provide man with a feeling that there is something constraining him without necessarily regulating him. "The only decentralization which would make possible the multiplication of the centers of communal life without weakening national unity is what might be called *occupational decentralization*" (390). The corporation, the labor union, the professional association, all must acquire a moral individuality. "We must seek in the past the germs of new life which it contained, and hasten their development" (391). Although Durkheim expressed these latter formulations more as a hope than as a prediction, it is clear that the problems he envisioned have materialized and that the solution he offered, the establishment of new communal solidarities along occupational lines, has become one solution to the problem of societal integration in a highly urbanized society.

MODERN VARIANTS OF EVOLUTIONARY THEORY

The importance of Durkheim and Spencer is evident when one considers modern evolutionists, most of whom borrowed heavily from these two sociologists. This is particularly true of modernization theories.

Modernization or Diachronic Theories of Unilinear Change

Modernization theories are concerned with the correlates of industrialization. While some claim to explain the processes whereby preindustrial societies became industrial, most are content to paint a before-and-after picture, contrasting a set of characteristics associated with preindustrial societies with the corresponding set that evolves in those that are highly industrialized. The theories are said to be diachronic, therefore, in that they attempt to infer process from a methodology of comparative statics. They are held to be unilinear in that all societies are held to undergo a parallel series of transformations during the process of industrialization that results in a highly homogeneous final product. Modernization is thus held to be universal in impact and highly predictable with regard to end product:

> We are confronted—whether for good or for bad —with a universal social solvent. The patterns of the relatively modernized societies, once developed, have shown a universal tendency to penetrate any social context whose participants have come in contact with them. . . . The patterns always penetrate; once the penetration has begun, the previous indigenous patterns always change; and they always change in the direction of some of the patterns of the relatively modernized societies (Levy, 1967: 190).

The definitions of modernization are numerous, but all relate in some way to the process or characteristics of industrialization. Thus, Levy (190) defines modernization directly in terms of technology: "I would consider any society the more modernized the greater the ratio of inanimate to animate power sources and the greater the extent to which human efforts are multiplied by the use of tools." [11] Smelser, applying the term somewhat more generically than Levy, defines it in terms of the characteristics it is hypothesized to be associated with. First, modernization is said to be conceptually related to (but more comprehensive than) economic development, by which Smelser (1966: 110–111) means

> . . . at least four distinct but interrelated processes . . . (1) In the realm of technology, a developing society is changing *from* simple and traditionalized techniques *toward* the application of scientific knowledge. (2) In agriculture, the developing society evolves *from* subsistence farming *toward* the commercial production of agricultural goods. This means specialization in cash crops, purchase of nonagricultural products in the market, and often agricultural wage labor. (3) In industry, the developing society undergoes a transition *from* the use of human and animal power *toward* industrialization proper, or men working for wages at power-driven machines, which produce commodities marketed outside the community of production. (4) In ecological arrangements, the developing society moves *from* the farm and village *toward* urban concentrations. Furthermore, while these four processes often occur simultaneously during development, this is not always so.

Modernization, then, includes economic development, and much more:

> The term "modernization"—a conceptual cousin of the term "economic development," but more comprehensive in scope—refers to the fact that technical, economic, and ecological changes ramify through the whole social and cultural fabric.

[11] This definition is also shared by Sahlins (see section on neoevolutionary theories).

In an emerging nation, we may expect profound changes (1) in the *political* sphere as simple tribal or village authority systems give way to systems of suffrage, political parties, representation, and civil service bureaucracies; (2) in the *educational* sphere, as the society strives to reduce illiteracy and increase economically productive skills; (3) in the religious sphere, as secularized belief systems begin to replace traditionalistic religions; (4) in the *familial* sphere, as extended kinship units lose their pervasiveness; (5) in the stratificational sphere, as geographical and social mobility tended to loosen fixed, ascriptive hierarchical systems (111).

Moore (1963: 89, 91–92), somewhat more directly, defines modernization as involving the

. . . "total" transformation of a traditional or pre-modern society into the types of technology and associated social organization that characterize the "advanced," economically prosperous, and relatively politically stable nations of the Western World. . . . In fact, we may . . . speak of the process as industrialization. Industrialization means the extensive use of inanimate sources of power for economic production, and all that entails by way of organization, transportation, communication, and so on.

Moore's definition, then, is close to Levy's. Other authors reviewed have little to say regarding the definition of modernization, the presumption apparently being that its meaning will become clear through the context. Thus Etzioni (1964: 253–257), in his introduction to the section of his book entitled "Modernization," neither defines the term nor attempts a synthesis of definitions of modernization, the subject matter of the following six chapters. Millikan and Blackmer (1961) offer no definition in their book on the emerging nations, nor does Lerner (1958: 45), except to note its kinship to earlier "Europeanization," "Americanization," and "Westernization," and to note that whatever its source, "modernization poses the same basic challenge—the infusion of a rationalist and positivist spirit. . . ."

In general, scholars have failed to define modernization. To accept Smelser's definition, in terms of the characteristics hypothesized to be associated with modernization, the assertion that such characteristics are correlates of modernization is true by definition and hence can be neither proved nor disproved. Actually, most writers, Smelser included, appear to have an essentially technological definition of modernization ultimately in mind, insofar as modernization is held to be part and process of industrialization. Levy's definition seems to have the greatest explanatory potential inasmuch as it predicts a set of social, economic, and political consequences attendant on changes in the ratio of inanimate to animate power sources, and thus avoids circularity.

For purposes of discussion, works dealing with modernization will be organized according to whether their principal focus is social or economic.

Levy and Smelser are both functionalists who have worked with, and been influenced by, Talcott Parsons. Levy worked with Parsons prior to Parsons' and Bales' development of the AGIL schema (see below) of functional prerequisites for social systems; his work on modernization incorporates many concepts postulated by Parsons around the time of the development of the pattern variables. Much of Smelser's empirical research is built around the Parsonsian AGIL schema; his work is thus representative of a later stage in the development of systems theory. Levy (1967: 189–208) provides us with a checklist of the correlates of modernization.[12] He does so on the basis of a binary distinction between "relatively" modernized societies and "relatively" nonmodernized societies.[13] "Modernized" is qualified to indicate that characteristics of each type are present in the other type; what is crucial is the degree to which a

[12] Levy (1967: 189–208) is a condensed version of *Modernization and the Structure of Society* (1965).

[13] The defining criterion of modernization—the ratio of inanimate to animate power—has previously been discussed.

given set of characteristics is widely shared by the people
in a given society. Levy holds that all relatively nonmodern
societies are more alike than they are like relatively modern
societies: the United States of the 18th century more closely
resembles the Togo of today than it does the United States
of today. Furthermore, the variation in societal types is reduced in modernization, as all societies increasingly come
to resemble one another.[14] Levy's checklist can be summarized as follows:

Foci of differences between relatively modernized and relatively non-modernized societies	Relatively Modernized Society	Relatively Nonmodernized Society
(1) specialization of organizations: specialized orientation to a single aspect of behavior	vast majority operate continually in such contexts ("compartmentalization")	relatively few operate in such contexts
(2) interdependency	high (low self-sufficiency)	low (high self-sufficiency)
(3) relationship emphases (dominant patterns)	rationality universalism; functional specificity;	tradition; particularism; functional diffuseness
(4) patterns of centralization	relatively high degree of centralization necessary and feasible	relatively low degree of centralization necessary and feasible

[14] This theme is also treated in W. Moore and A. Feldman (1960:
364): "Thus industrialization is viewed as a process that creates
cultural homogeneity, in that certain patterns of belief and behavior
are necessarily common to all industrial societies. Moreover, com-
monality is not limited to the single act or norm but applies as well
to the configurations into which they are formed, for example, the
interrelations among machine technology, division of labor, and au-
thoritative coordination."

(5) generalized media of exchange and markets	generalization of media of exchange, & use of money in general, are high and increasing; extensive and increasing use of markets	low generalization and limited use of money; limited use of markets
(6) bureaucracy	widespread and specialized	limited
(7) family considerations	important, but decreasing amounts of social control, education, role preparation, and general orientation occur in a family context	important; major social control, learning, role preparation, and general orientation occur in family context
(8) town-village interdependencies	urban, industrial, with main flow of goods and services (and know-how) from urban to rural contexts	rural, agricultural, with main flow of goods & services from rural to urban contexts (rents, taxes, interest profits)

Among other things, Levy goes on to consider the implications of his distinctions in terms of problems of strains and control. He also delineates some of the advantages and disadvantages that accrue to being a latecomer to the modernization process. The advantages include the possibility of borrowing technologies, of skipping stages, of obtaining assistance, etc., while the disadvantages include problems of scale (competing with modernized societies), conversion (of resources from one use to another), and disappointment. Levy, of course, feels that modernizing nations must, by and large, progress through the stages experienced by a relatively modern society during its period of industrialization. Although he does not discuss actual processes, he makes it clear that the patterns associated with modernized societies are always destructive of those associated with nonmodern systems. The theme of recapitulation is common in the literature, with most writers arguing that in all important aspects of industrialization, a recapitulation of the "European model," but with greater central planning, is essential (see, for example, Holton, 1960; Apter, 1960; Kerr, 1960; Parsons, 1960).

Smelser (1964: 258–274; 1966) focuses more on process than does Levy, noting the interplay between structural differentiation and integration and the social disturbances caused by the lag between the two. "Differentiation refers to the evolution from a multifunctional role structure to several more specialized structures" (1964: 261). Smelser discusses differentiation of economic, family, value, and stratification spheres. Economic differentiation, for example, refers to reallocation of the production function from the family to specialized institutions (factories, commercialized farms). Differentiation of exchange systems (markets with generalized media of exchange replace simple trade systems) is another example. In this treatment, Smelser and Levy strongly resemble one another. Smelser goes beyond Levy in tracing the impact of such differentiation on the family which, stripped of its economic (and educational, and religious, etc.) functions, becomes increasingly specialized in social-emotional gratification. If the traditional family is structured along lines of economic production (marriages arranged for economic security, etc.), ideally, the modern family is built around conjugal love. With regard to stratification, Smelser notes, differentiation means that other (achieved) evaluative standards intrude on ascribed memberships and individual mobility increases (indicating differentiation of one's functional position from its point of origin). All of the structural differentiation that occurs during the process of modernization raises the problem of reintegration, as Durkheim so clearly illustrated in his criticism of Spencer's laissez-faire attitude towards regulation (see previous discussion). Thus, new integrative mechanisms, which are themselves a product of differentiation, arise (i.e., their functions were previously performed in nonspecialized structures such as the family or the church). Examples of integrative mechanisms that arise in the economic sphere (where most economic functions have been sheared from the family) include labor recruitment agencies and exchanges, labor unions, government, in its regulation of labor allocation, welfare agencies, cooperatives, and savings institutions. Voluntary associations integrate the community; parties and interest groups integrate the polity. Unfortunately, these integrative mechanisms do not always keep apace with the rapid differentiation that is occurring and social disturbances result.

Smelser enumerates several sources of disturbance. (1) Structural change is uneven during modernization, producing anomie (in Durkheim's sense of deregulation: the old rules no longer apply). For example, "in colonial societies . . . the European powers frequently revolutionized the economic and political framework . . . but at the same time encouraged or imposed a conservatism in traditional religions, class, and family systems" (1966: 119). The imbalance between industrial and agricultural development also falls into this category of disturbances. (2) New activities and norms often conflict with the old; new kinds of social and economic activities conflict with traditional activities. (3) The attempts of the central government to deal with modernization in general and unrest in particular may itself be a source of unrest, as traditional (often local) power sources resist encroachment from the center.

Although Levy does not speak specifically in terms of the tension created by differentiation and integration, it is clear that he has this tension in mind when he considers problems of modernization. Thus, Levy (1967: 204) discusses such problems as "changes in fit" (e.g., "the teaching of new techniques undermining general family control," akin to Smelser's first source of disturbance), "fundamentalist reactions" (Smelser's second source of disturbances), and "the problem of adequate knowledge" (referring to the knowledge necessary for necessary centralized planning,

which relates to Smelser's third source of disturbances—
the inability of the government to exercise adequate central
control). Both Levy and Smelser are agreed on the need for
increased central control during modernization.

Although their terminology is somewhat different, it is
clear that Levy and Smelser both regard society as a
mechanistic system. In this system, new structures are developed to perform the functions of those that are no longer
performing adequately, and when this process of structural
differentiation proceeds unevenly, tensions and imbalances
are created for the system as a whole (which imbalances
are themselves dealt with by the creation of new, integrative mechanisms).[15]

A related conceptualization of the character of modernization—from the anthropological literature—is Redfield's folk-urban continuum. Redfield, like Levy, sets up
two ideal polar types which define the end points of a modernization process. Most of Redfield's work is concerned
with the folk end of the continuum: the urban end is defined residually. He (1947: 294) describes folk society as

> . . . small, isolated, nonliterate, and homogeneous,
> with a strong sense of group solidarity. The ways
> of living are conventionalized into that coherent
> system which we call a "culture." Behavior is
> traditional, spontaneous, uncritical, and personal;
> there is no legislation or habit of experiment and
> reflection for intellectual ends. Kinship, its re-
> lationships and institutions, are the type cate-
> gories of experience and the familial group is the
> unit of action. The sacred prevails over the secu-
> lar; the economy is one of status rather than the
> market.

Social change is said to result from "increase of contacts,
bringing about heterogeneity and disorganization of culture," (1941: 369) among other things. There is, however,

[15] Levy discusses several ways to reintegrate society, including
the "creative use of the armed forces," alterations of town-village
imbalances, fomenting nationalism, using politics as recreation, and
Fallers' "trickle effect." Smelser's integrative mechanisms were dealt
with previously in the text. For an empirical analysis, see Smelser
(1959).

"no single necessary cause of secularization and individualization" (369). As an example of change, Oscar Lewis' (1930) restudy of Tepoztlán indicates that the introduction of plow culture (as opposed to hoe culture, or *tlacolol*) resulted in "population density, family cooperation, market economy, group solidarity, and conflicts indicative of social disorganization. What is more, this heterogeneity of technique seems to be related to shifts in the other variables away from the folk and, hence, towards the urban type" (Miner, 1964: 152). The folk-urban construction is not without its problems. These are grouped by Miner (152) into three categories—which, of course, apply to all ideal type constructs. First, there is the problem of fit between empirical evidence and the ideal type construct. Do societies "hang together" as predicted by the ideal types? Does change in some of the ideal type variables produce change in the predicted direction among all others? Is movement generally from the folk to the urban pole? Lewis' study raises doubts about all of these points. Second, how adequately are the ideal type characteristics defined and operationalized? Miner concludes that the answer thus far has been "not very." Certainly, many of the differences between Redfield's and Lewis' studies can be attributed to their differing definitions and operationalization of constructs. Finally, how much theoretical insight does the folk-urban concept provide? Murdock (1943: 133–136), Herskovits (1948: 604–607), and Lewis (quotations from 1930: 432–440) have criticized the folk-urban concept as being ahistorical, afunctional, apsychological, and excessively formal (rather than concerned with process). One is tempted to conclude that Redfield offers little beyond the Spencerian insight that increased population density produces greater differentiation (heterogeneity, in Redfield's terms).

Moore (1963: ch. 5) synthesizes many of the previous works in his discussion of the conditions, consequences, and dynamics of modernization.[16] He may be summarized as follows:

[16] For another attempt at synthesis, see Wilensky and Lebeaux (1965). This work applies theories of social change to a description

I. Industrialization: Conditions

  A. Values: ". . . extensive value changes are the most fundamental condition for economic transformation." These include:
    =the value of economic growth, involving:
      —high individual mobility
      —achievement rather than ascription in role allocation
    =national integration or identification (nationalism or mobilization)

  B. Institutions:
    1. economic
      a. property: must be transferable (permits mobilization of the factors of production)
      b. labor: must be geographically and socially mobile
      c. exchange: markets and generalized media
    2. political stability
      a. reliable and just legal system
      b. simple civil order
    3. rationality: problem-solving orientation and dedication to deliberate change (the entrepreneur)

  C. Organization:
    1. specialized and hierarchical bureaucracy
    2. appropriate fiscal organization of state (banking, taxation)

  D. Motivation
    1. achievement orientation
    2. innovative personality

II. Industrialization: concomitants and consequences:

  A. In the economic structure:
    1. incorporating subsistence agricultural sector

---

of the United States in the late 19th and 20th centuries, tracing the impact of industrialization on the economy and on the family. A discussion of "urbanism as a way of life" modifies Wirth in light of current developments in primary group relations in the United States.

into commercialized market system of the national economy = reduction of proportion of population in agriculture

2. long-term upgrading of minimum and average skill levels in the labor force
3. high degree of labor mobility
4. lateral extension of occupations
5. reinvestment of profits
6. universal extension and commercialization of the market for consumer goods
7. expanding range of goods produced; services eventually occupy a higher proportion of consumer expenditures
8. increasing specialization and interdependence in economic structure

B. Demographic and ecological structure:
1. demographic transition precedes industrialization—at least with regard to declining mortality. Result:
2. high levels of population growth (hindering economic growth)
3. family planning will follow modernization rather than precede it
4. high birth rates and reduced infant mortality will produce "young" populations (taxing educational facilities)
5. overurbanization reflects uneven economic development between city and country
6. service sector (manned, marginally, by immigrants) expands more rapidly than industrial—contrary to Western experience

C. Social structure: although some variation in the "social consequences" of modernization is possible, Moore feels essentially that ". . . economic modernization does have some invariant implications for *social structure* and imposes rather sharp limits on the variation of some other features of social organization":
1. " 'corporate' kin groups, acting as economic and political entities, will not survive the

impact of a modernizing economy, but remnants of reciprocity are likely to remain"

2. the breakdown of traditional patterns (along with the incomplete establishment of new institutions) will produce extensive "family disorganization"

3. voluntary marriages will replace arranged ones, and generational strains will reflect the increased training that children receive away from home

4. the family will become specialized in consuming (as the production function is stripped away from the family)

5. the role of woman will change, as she becomes more involved in supervising children and disposing family income, and possibly less involved in production

6. informal social controls will be weakened (in the heterogeneous city) and formal agencies will be required

7. rapid change and shearing of old ties will produce apathy and alienation

8. education will become widespread and performed in specialized institutions

9. mass communication will break down village isolation and result in mobilization of national political consciousness

10. differentiation between work and leisure will occur

11. specialized interest groups and associations will proliferate

12. secular attitudes will reflect the institutionalization of rationality, but some religious orientation will survive

13. competing systems of social stratification will emerge, resulting in polarization between innovative-directing elements and unskilled reluctant participants. This polarization will diminish over time as intermediate and lateral positions are created

14. mobilization of the populace will be necessary—be it through manipulation or voluntary participation
15. administratively, the rational bureaucracy
will emerge

III. The dynamics of industrial societies:

A. Restoration of traditional patterns:
1. the conjugal family replaces the consan-
guineal family at early stages, since "the
consanguine principle of familial organization, is clearly inconsistent with individual
mobility on merit". But later on, kinship
claims reassert themselves, as families come
again to serve a function of support (financial, bereavement), while allowing for status differences among family units
2. impersonal markets which characterize the
early stages may become somewhat more
personal (knowing your grocer?)
B. Processes of continuous change: some processes never reverse direction such as specialization (or role differentiation: the number of distinguishable occupations continues to increase)
C. Organization of change: an increasing amount
of change becomes deliberate or planned—
change becomes organized and institutional
D. Divergence among industrial societies: sources
of divergence among societies during the
course of modernization include:
1. different and persistent antecedent conditions
2. different enduring social tensions and their
effects
3. possibility of borrowing technology and
social form from other (more advanced)
nations
4. the final product is itself not stable; industrial societies are themselves changing, and

so may industrializing nations diverge also
5. marked differences in political regimes exist
   in industrial societies and probably will
   persist in industrializing societies

In his discussion of conditions and consequences, Moore adds little to what has been previously discussed, except to specify some of the economic characteristics of industrialization. His discussion of conditions departs from Max Weber (1964) and Talcott Parsons (1960), although he does raise the question of motivation.[17] Again, his discussion of consequences, particularly social, consists primarily in elaborations on the theme of differentiation and specialization. His predictions, however, are somewhat more specific than those encountered previously. Moore quite clearly feels that little variation is possible in the process of industrialization and in this, most other writers concur, although some argue for greater flexibility with regard to specific institutions or rates and sequences of change.[18] When one looks to Moore for a discussion of processes, however, one is somewhat disappointed. The discussion of the dynamics of industrial societies is general and descriptive and fails to satisfy what Moore (1963: 106) himself recognizes to be a critical need: ". . . structural analysis is used to trace through the consequences of the new set of social elements, but only rarely is attention given to the interactions of structures in juxtaposition. . . ."

Moore touched on economic and psychological aspects of modernization. These two themes constitute distinct bodies of literature which cannot be reviewed in detail in this book. Nonetheless, brief mention of several works from the economic development literature that seem particularly relevant will be made. Millikan and Blackmer (1961) iden-

---

[17] "Achievement motivation and social change" is not discussed in this book. See David C. McClelland (1967); also Everett E. Hagen (1962).

[18] Manning Nash (1960) and Bert F. Hoselitz (1960: 217–237), for example, argue that the alleged subversion of the extended kinship system by industrialism has not been empirically demonstrated. See also chapters by Singer, Belshaw, Hammond, and Herskovitz in Moore and Feldman (1960).

tify several preconditions for cumulative economic growth. These include expansion of human resources, output of basic social overhead capital, and radical transformation in the agricultural sector.[19] Human resources are developed by literacy, education, and specialized manpower programs. Such programs are generally not remunerative when they are initiated and must have been in effect for some time before trained people become available in adequate numbers. Similarly, social overhead capital (basic transport, communication, power, and irrigation facilities) must also be developed early. Many such facilities cannot be imported but must be developed at home; they tend to be large scale or "lumpy" (high capital-output ratios), and they require a long period of gestation before return is realized. "For all these reasons, if development is to be accelerated, very substantial investment must be undertaken in social overhead capital during the early period of development" (Moore, 1963: 51). Finally, agricultural development must keep apace with industrial growth if effective development is to be achieved, as food scarcity turns the terms of trade against industry (and may even result in spending scarce foreign exchange for the importation of food).[20] Once these preconditions have been realized for some time, the country will be economically ready for the "big push" (Leibenstein, 1957; Rostow, 1961) into self-sustained growth.[21] "Essential for

[19] For a more technical but still fairly elementary discussion, see Charles P. Kindleberger (1965).

[20] There is by no means agreement on these points, which generally argue in favor of balanced growth. Thus, Hirschman (1958) argues that "leapfrogging" may be the most productive use of scarce investment resources, assuming the investment to be in what Hirschman calls "directly productive activities" (DPA)—those with high forward and backward linkages to other sectors of the economy, which will thereby induce growth in those linked sectors. Hirschman further argues that DPA investment should precede social overhead capital investment, presumably since the latter will of necessity follow if it is really needed. Most economists disagree. R. Nurske (1953), for example, argues for balanced growth on the demand side, while W. Arthur Lewis (1955) argues for balanced growth on the supply side.

[21] The "big push" theme is a recurrent one in the economic literature. Harvey Leibenstein (1957), for example, argues that backwards economies are in a "quasi-stable equilibrium" situation, in which income always fluctuates around a subsistence level; developed

the assurance of self-sustaining growth is a sharp rise in the fraction of national income devoted to capital formation" (Millikan and Blackmer, 1961: 55). Key industrial sectors will take the lead, depending on the resources and technology of the nation. Railroads (England), timber (Sweden), and import-substitution industries (Argentina, Mexico, India) are examples. The government may find it necessary to insure adequate levels of investment, either by taxing consumption, providing tax incentives for investment, or undertaking the investment itself. Market imperfections, particularly in the area of investment allocation, require that ". . . in a contemporary take-off, government programming and administration of a number of important processes and relationships is essential" (57). Agricultural reform (expropriation) will also be necessary. Importation of foreign capital may also help, although it is not absolutely necessary.

The concept of the "big push" has been used by economists to explain the transition from an essentially static, subsistence-level economy to a "modern" one, characterized by continuous growth in per capita income. This conceptualization of the problem closely parallels the sociological concept of modernization as consisting of two poles, with a transitional phase between. The economic approach differs from the sociological in two crucial respects, however. (1) It does not err in regarding the "modern" or "urban" pole of the continuum as an essentially static ideal type, a goal to be realized. Rather, it holds that modern societies are themselves characterized by change—in this case, continual movement in the direction of ever-expanding output. Two essentially different theoretical constructs apply to the "before" and "after" stages, a two-sector stagnation model on the one hand (W. A. Lewis, 1954), and a growth model on the other. (2) It has something to say about the transi-

economies are "dynamic" or "nonequilibrium" economies, characterized by continual growth; and that a "critical minimum effort" (i.e., a "big push") is necessary to raise per capita income to a point where growth will be self-sustaining. W. W. Rostow (1961) argues the same position in his concept of the "take-off," considered below in this chapter.

tional phase, however inadequately, with regard to the precise mechanisms involved in the "big push." W. W. Rostow (1961; 1964: 275–290) has elaborated the most popularized version of the "big push" theory by conceptualizing the transitional period in terms of an analogy to an airplane: this is the period of "take-off" into "self-sustained growth." Assuming the preconditions have been met (these are essentially the same as those delineated by Millikan and Blackmer above), ". . . the forces which have [previously] yielded marginal bursts of activity now expand and become quantitatively significant as rapid-moving trends" (1964: 279). A particular stimulus will occur (a political revolution, a technological innovation, a newly favorable international environment) and society will be ready for it with an overall higher rate of productive investment. Investment, indeed, is the key to the Rostownian (281) model:

> For the present purpose, the take-off is defined as requiring all three of the following related conditions:
>   (a) a rise in the rate of productive investment from (say) 5 per cent or less to over 10 per cent of national income (or net national product);
>   (b) the development of one or more substantial manufacturing sectors, with a high rate of growth;
>   (c) the existence or quick emergence of a political, social, and institutional framework which exploits the impulses to expansion in the modern sector and the potential external economy effects of the take-off and gives to growth an on-going character.

Investment funds may come from several sources, including income shifts from those who spend less productively to those who spend more productively (as in the case of Meiji Japan), from governmental confiscatory and taxation devices, and from the ploughback of profits in rapidly expanding sectors. How adequate is Rostow's argument? Points (b) and (c) clearly lack specificity; words such as "substantial manufacturing sector," "high rate of growth," and "political, social, and institutional framework which exploits the impulses to expansion" mean little except by way of hindsight. More significant is Kuznets' (1965: 232) assertion that "the doubling of capital investment proportions and the implicit sharp acceleration in the rate of growth of national product . . . are not confirmed by the statistical evidence for those countries on his list for which we have data." Kuznets further argues that there is no empirical distinction between the take-off stages and the immediately preceding and succeeding stages and that specific characteristics of individual countries (historical heritage, time of entry into growth process, or degree of backwardness) are not given adequate weight. Thus, it would appear that to the degree Rostow specifies conditions, he is not supported by the data.

Aspects of Functionalism and Systems Theory: Adaptive Upgrading

The evolutionary aspects of contemporary functionalist theory have been largely covered in previous sections, particularly in discussions of Spencer and Durkheim and of Levy and Smelser. The principal link between evolutionism and functionalism is the concept of differentiation, by which is meant the development of functionally specialized societal structures. This is analogous to the evolution of highly complex specialized organisms that consist of numerous interdependent and specialized organs. No sociologist has carried this line of thinking further than Talcott Parsons, who conceives society as a social system functioning within a larger action system comprised of subsystems. For Parsons (1966: esp. 28–29), all action systems perform four essential functions—adaptation, goal-attainment, integration, and latent pattern maintenance (AGIL). Within the larger action system, the social system performs the function of integration (adaptation is performed by the behavioral organism, goal attainment by the personality system, and pattern maintenance by the cultural system). Within the social system, the societal community performs the function of integration; adaptation is the function of the economy, goal attainment of the polity, and pattern maintenance of specialized structures such as the family and religious entities. As societies evolve, they differentiate along AGIL lines—first along the lines specified above, then into subsystems of each AGIL function (polity subsystems, economy subsystems, etc.). *Primitive* societies are highly undifferentiated, but the emergence of a stratification system (promoted by inequitable distribution of resources and kinship intermarriage) and the differentiation of specialized religious institutions result in subsystems specialized in pattern maintenance (religion) and goal-attainment (chieftains). With the emergence of literacy, *archaic intermediate* societies come into being. In AGIL terms, the integration function is differentiated from the pattern maintenance function, as the emergent cosmological religion is managed by a priestly class. *Advanced intermediate* societies are characterized by full adult male literacy, cosmological religion, and an institutionalized legal code (which integrates the societal community). Finally, *modern* societies presuppose industrial technology and are characterized by a high degree of specialization, institutionalization of property, and other characteristics outlined by Smelser earlier in this chapter. From an evolutionary perspective, the important thing is that change is continual through differentiation in a process of adaptive upgrading:

> If differentiation is to yield a more balanced, evolved system, each newly differentiated substructure . . . must have increased adaptive capacity for performing its *primary* function, as compared to the performance of *that* function in the previous, more diffuse structure. Thus economic production is typically more efficient in factories than in households. We may call this process the *adaptive upgrading* aspect of the evolutionary change cycle. It applies to both role and collectivity levels (22). . . .

> Among change processes, the type most important to the evolutionary perspective is the *enhancement of adaptive capacity*, either within the society originating a new type of structure or,

> through cultural diffusion and the involvement of
> other factors with the new type of structure,
> within other societies and perhaps at later pe-
> riods (21). . . .
>
> Our perspective clearly involves evolutionary
> judgments—for example, that intermediate so-
> cieties are more advanced than primitive societies.
> . . . I have tried to make my basic criterion con-
> gruent with that used in biological theory, calling
> more "advanced" the systems that display greater
> generalized adaptive capacity (110).

Following contemporary biological thought, then, Parsons does not hold with Spencer that all societies emerged
from a single primitive type. Rather, "the evidence we have
reviewed indicates that, in the earlier stages of evolution,
there have been *multiple* and *variable* origins of the *basic*
societal types" (110). There has been considerable variability and branching along evolutionary lines, a point raised
with regard to biological evolution earlier.[22]

Neoevolutionary Theories: Multilinear Evolution, General and Specific Evolution

Evolutionary theories in the social sciences, at least
those which call themselves such, have recently enjoyed a
revival, largely through the works of Steward, White,
Sahlins, and Service (see also Dobzhansky, 1955; 1962;
Tax, 1959). All of these writers have attempted to come
to grips with the great cultural diversity noted by sociologists and anthropologists in the years following Spencer's
works on evolution, a diversity which had long discredited
evolutionary theories *qua* evolutionary theories.

Steward's (1959; 1964) argument has been termed
"multilinear evolution" and is summarized in the proposition that "the facts now accumulated indicate that human
culture evolved along a number of different lines; we must
think of evolution not as unilinear but multilinear." The
ecological area in which a particular culture develops neces-
sitates a distinctive form of life. The task of the anthro-

[22] See discussion of Stebbins (1967) article.

pologist is to identify culture types within which distinctive lines of evolution emerge. Thus, one type of culture area produces hunters, another an agricultural civilization. "Human evolution, then, is not merely a matter of biology, but of the interaction of man's physical and cultural characteristics, each influencing the other" (1964: 139). Multilinear evolution is more of a methodology than a coherent set of propositions, and, in fact, its principal task appears to be taxonomy rather than explanation. If it avoids the historicism which characterized earlier evolutionary theories, it also fails to come to grips adequately with the task of theoretical generalization.

Sahlins (Sahlins and Service, 1960: 12–44) sees evolution as encompassing *both* diversity and cumulative change (progress). To Sahlins (12–13),

> It appears almost obvious upon stating it that in both its biological and cultural spheres evolution moves simultaneously in two directions. On one side, it creates diversity through adaptive modification: new forms differentiate from old. On the other side, evolution generates progress: higher forms arise from, and surpass, lower. The first of these directions is Specific Evolution, and the second, General Evolution. But note that specific and general evolution are not different concrete realities; they are rather aspects of the same total process, which is also to say, two contexts in which we may place the same evolutionary things and events.

Sahlins agrees with Steward that adaptation to specific conditions, including the previous cultural heritage of a society, results in tremendous cultural diversity among societies. "New cultural traits arising through adaptation can be considered adaptive advances" (25). Unlike specific biological evolution, specific cultural evolution allows for the possibility of transmitting variation through diffusion. "Separate cultural traditions unlike separate biological lineages, may converge by coalescence" (27). Furthermore, cultures may borrow wholesale the achievements of other cultures without recapitulating all the stages of development. Thus, specific evolution provides a link to understanding seemingly discontinuous progress in the general evolution to higher forms. Specific evolution "is the phylogenic, ramifying, historic passage of a culture along its many lines, the adaptive modification of particular cultures" (38). What, then, are the criteria for progress—for general evolution? Sahlins (35) identifies three. First, there is the passage from less to greater energy transformation: "It seems to us that progress is the total transformation of energy involved in the creation and perpetuation of a cultural organization." [23] Related to this is the second criterion, passage from lower to higher levels of integration. "As in life, thermodynamic achievement [passage from lower to higher energy levels] has its organizational counterpart, higher levels of integration. Cultures that transform more energy have more parts and subsystems, more specialization of parts, and more effective means of integration of the whole" (35–36).[24] This results in the third criterion, greater adaptability. "General progress can also be viewed as improvement in 'all-around adaptability.' Higher cultural forms tend to dominate and replace lower, and the range of dominance is proportionate to the degree of progress. So modern national culture tends to spread around the globe (37). . . ." [25] Sahlins has comprehended Steward's more limited taxonomizing (Sahlins might term it "phylogenizing") and, in the interest of capturing cultural diversity and clarifying the explanation with regard to cumulative progress characterizing the organismic theorists, both specific and general evolution have been related within a single theoretical framework. If individual societies develop along highly variable lines, according to considera-

[23] Note the similarity between this definition of general cultural evolution and Levy's definition of modernization.

[24] This, of course, is the organismic argument, from Spencer and Durkheim to modern functionalists such as Parsons, Smelser, and Levy, but with an interesting twist: whereas the sociological tradition has emphasized differentiation as the criterion of evolutionary change, with integration regarded more as problematic, Sahlins emphasizes integration as the criterion.

[25] This criterion is equivalent to Parsons' notion of "adaptive upgrading" and is compatible with related concepts in cultural and human ecology.

tions of environment, previous cultural tradition, and so
forth, they also develop in the general direction of progress,
with the cultural forms characteristic of highly energized,
integrated, and adaptable societies replacing those of societies that are not as well developed. Here, then, is a framework capable of accommodating both organismic and modernization theories, indeed, all theories which claim to have
an evolutionary perspective.

REFERENCES

Apter, David.
  1960   "Political organization and ideology." In Wilbert
         E. Moore and Arnold S. Feldman (eds.), Labor
         Commitment and Social Change in Developing
         Areas. New York: Social Science Research Coun-
         cil.
Comte, Auguste.
  1875   System of Positive Polity. Vol. 2, "Social statics."
         London: Longmans, Green.
  1893   The Positive Philosophy. Vol. 2. London: Kegan
         Paul, Trench, Trubner and Company.
  1964   "General appendix: Early essays." In Amitai and
         Eva Etzioni (eds.), Social Change. New York:
         Basic Books.
Darwin, Charles.
  1859   Origin of Species. New York: D. Appleton.
  1880   The Descent of Man. New York: D. Appleton.
Darwin, Francis.
  1887   The Life and Letters of Charles Darwin. New
         York: D. Appleton.
Dobzhansky, Theodosius.
  1955   Evolution, Genetics and Man. New York: Wiley.
  1962   Mankind Evolving. New Haven, Conn.: Yale Uni-
         versity Press.
Durkheim, Emile.
  1951   Suicide. New York: Free Press.
  1964a The Division of Labor in Society. New York: Free
         Press.

1964b The Rules of Sociological Method. New York: Free
       Press.

Etzioni, Amitai, and Eva Etzioni, eds.
1964   Social Change, New York: Basic Books.

Hagen, Everett E.
1962   On the Theory of Social Change. Homewood, Ill.:
       Dorsey.

Herskovits, Melville J.
1948   Man and His Works. New York: Knopf.

Hirschman, Albert O.
1958   The Strategy of Economic Development. New
       Haven, Conn.: Yale University Press.

Holton, Richard H.
1960   "Changing demand and consumption." In Wilbert
       E. Moore and Arnold S. Feldman (eds.), Labor
       Commitment and Social Change in Developing
       Areas. New York: Social Science Research Coun-
       cil.

Hoselitz, Bert F.
1960   "The market matrix." In Wilbert E. Moore and
       Arnold S. Feldman (eds.), Labor Commitment and
       Social Change in Developing Areas. New York:
       Social Science Research Council.

Huxley, Julian.
1942   Evolution, the Modern Synthesis. New York:
       Harper & Row.

Kerr, Clark.
1960   "Changing Social Structures." In Wilbert E.
       Moore and Arnold S. Feldman (eds.), Labor Com-
       mitment and Social Change in Developing Areas.
       New York: Social Science Research Council.

Kindleberger, Charles P.
1965   Economic Development. New York: McGraw-Hill.

Kuznets, Simon.
1965   Economic Growth and Structure. New York: W.
       W. Norton.

Leibenstein, Harvey.
1957   Economic Backwardness and Economic Growth.
       Cambridge: University Press.

Lerner, Daniel.
  1958   The Passing of Traditional Society. New York:
          Free Press.
Levy, Marion J.
  1965   Modernization and the Structure of Society. 2 vols.
          Princeton, N.J.: Princeton University Press.
  1967   "Social patterns (structures) and problems of
          modernization." In Wilbert E. Moore and Robert
          M. Cook. (eds.), Readings on Social Change.
          Englewood Cliffs, N.J.: Prentice-Hall.
Lewis, W. Arthur.
  1954   "Economic development with unlimited supplies
          of labor." Manchester School (May) 1954.
  1955   The Theory of Economic Growth. Homewood, Ill.:
          Irwin.
Lewis, Oscar.
  1930   Life in a Mexican Village: Tepoztlán Restudied.
          Urbana: University of Illinois Press.
Linton, Ralph.
  1936   The Study of Man. New York: D. Appleton-Cen-
          tury.
McClelland, David C.
  1967   The Achieving Society. New York: Free Press.
Maine, Henry Sumner.
  1907   Ancient Law. London: John Murray.
Martindale, Don A.
  1960   The Nature and Types of Sociological Theory. Bos-
          ton: Houghton Mifflin.
Millikan, Max F., and Donald L. M. Blackmer.
  1961   The Emerging Nations: Their Growth and United
          States Policy. Boston: Little, Brown.
Miner, Horace.
  1964   "The folk-urban continuum." In Amitai and Eva
          Etzioni (eds.), Social Change. New York: Basic
          Books.
Moore, Wilbert E.
  1963   Social Change. Englewood Cliffs, N.J.: Prentice-
          Hall.
Moore, Wilbert E., and Robert M. Cook, eds.

1967   Readings on Social Change. Englewood Cliffs, N.J.: Prentice-Hall.

Moore, Wilbert E., and Arnold S. Feldman, eds.
1960   Labor Commitment and Social Change in Developing Areas. New York: Social Science Research Council.

Morgan, Lewis H.
1877   Ancient Society, or, Researches in the Lines of Human Progress from Savagery through Barbarism to Civilization. Chicago: H. Kerr.

Murdock, George P.
1943   "Review of 'Folk Culture of the Yucatan.'" American Anthropologist 14: 133–36.

Nash, Manning.
1960   "Kinship and voluntary association." In Wilbert E. Moore and Arnold S. Feldman (eds.), Labor Commitment and Social Change in Developing Areas. New York: Social Science Research Council.

Nurske, R.
1953   Problems of Capital Formation in Underdeveloped Areas. New York: Oxford University Press.

Parsons, Talcott.
1951   The Social System. New York: Free Press.
1960   Structure and Process in Modern Societies. Part 2, "Social structure and economic development." New York: Free Press.
1966   Societies: Evolutionary and Comparative Perspectives. Englewood Cliffs, N.J.: Prentice-Hall.

Parsons, Talcott, and Neil J. Smelser.
1956   Economy and Society. New York: Free Press.

Redfield, Robert.
1941   The Folk Culture of the Yucatan. Chicago: University of Chicago Press.
1947   "The folk society." American Journal of Sociology 52: 294.

Rostow, W. W.
1961   The Stages of Economic Growth. Cambridge: University Press.
1964   "The take-off into self-sustained growth." Pp.

275–290 in Amitai and Eva Etzioni (eds.), Social Change. New York: Basic Books.

Sahlins, Marshall D., and Elman R. Service, eds.
1960 Evolution and Culture. Ann Arbor: University of Michigan Press.

Simpson, G. G.
1949 The Meaning of Evolution. New Haven, Conn.: Yale University Press.

Smelser, Neil J.
1959 Social Change in the Industrial Revolution. Chicago: University of Chicago Press.
1964 "Toward a theory of modernization." In Amitai and Eva Etzioni (eds.), Social Change. New York: Basic Books.
1966 "The modernization of social relations." In Myron Weiner (ed.), Modernization. New York: Basic Books.

Spencer, Herbert.
1892 Sociology. Vol. 1. New York: D. Appleton.
1958 First Principles of a New System of Philosophy. New York: DeWitt Revolving Fund.
1964 "Sociology." In Amitai and Eva Etzioni (eds.), Social Change. New York: Basic Books.

Stebbins, G. Ledyard.
1967 "Pitfalls and guideposts in comparing organic and social evolution." In Wilbert E. Moore and Robert M. Cook (eds.), Readings on Social Change. Englewood Cliffs, N.J.: Prentice-Hall.

Steward, Julian H.
1959 Theory of Culture Change. Urbana: University of Illinois Press.
1964 "A neo-evolutionist approach." In Amitai and Eva Etzioni (eds.), Social Change. New York: Basic Books.

Tax, Sol, ed.
1959 Evolution After Darwin. Chicago: University of Chicago Press.

Toennies, Ferdinand.
1964 "Community and society: Gemeinschaft und Gesell-

schaft." In Amitai and Eva Etzioni (eds.), Social
Change. New York: Basic Books, 1964.
Weber, Max.
1964   The Theory of Social and Economic Organization.
New York: Free Press.
Weiner, Myron, ed.
1966   Modernization. New York: Basic Books.
Wilensky, Harold L., and Charles N. Lebeaux.
1965   Industrial Society and Social Welfare. New York:
Free Press.

2

Equilibrium Theory:
The Concept of Homeostasis

Homeostasis is a notion borrowed originally from me-
chanics and, more recently, from the biological sciences.
The term means "uniform state," and homeostatic mechanisms are mechanisms for reaching and maintaining uniform states. The central concept is that of equilibrium,
which can be defined with Homans (1950: 303–304) as a
condition of a system whereby "the state of the elements
that enter the system and of the mutual relationships between them is such that any small change in one of the
elements will be followed by changes in the other elements
tending to reduce the amount of that change." [1]

[1] This concept can be modified to include the possibility of a
moving equilibrium: "A social system is in moving equilibrium and
authority exists when the state of the elements that enter the system and of the relations between them, including the behavior of
the leader, is such that disobedience to the orders of the leader will
be followed by changes in the other elements tending to bring the
system back to the state the leader would have wished it to reach if
the disobedience had not taken place." (Homans; 1950: 422).

Parallels in the Biological Sciences

V. C. Wynne-Edwards (1962, as presented in Brown, 1965: 6–45) has proposed what can be called the homeostatic theory of the elementary forms of social organization. This theory holds that elementary social forms have evolved because they are means of attaining a population ideal in number and dispersion relative to food resources. These forms constitute homeostatic mechanisms. If one conceives of an optimum amount of food per individual for any given species and in a given foraging area, then, according to Wynne-Edwards, the elementary social practices of the species will all be means towards maintaining this optimum ratio of food per individual member. Two important social practices identified by Wynne-Edwards are territoriality and dominance. Territoriality is the process whereby the numbers of a species in any given locality are regulated via migration. Thus, starlings "calculate" the volume of food in a given area and the number of their species present; after population has been permitted to increase until the optimum food-number ratio is reached, birds will leave the territory to maintain the ratio. Dominance orders, of which the pecking order is an example, bestow the privilege of precedence in feeding and in mating. Dominance is often determined on the basis of symbolic or ritualistic competition, rather than in outright fighting: this suggests to Wynne-Edwards that the function of dominance is to insure group, rather than individual, survival (Brown, 1965: 21).

> The dominance order is, he suggests, a "social guillotine." Whenever food begins to be in short supply the tail end of the society is cut off and required to migrate or forego mating or even to starve. There is a kind of social contract to feed and mate and occupy space in a society from the top down, and so a shortage of resources does not lead to combat but to migration or reduced fertility or increased mortality in a foreordained segment. This is a good arrangement, not primarily because it favors individual specimens that are larger or more ferocious, but rather because it is a *peaceful convention* guaranteeing that *some* members of the group will endure.

In sum, territoriality, dominance, migration, fertility, and mortality serve as homeostatic social processes whereby an optimum food/individual ratio is maintained for a given species in a given habitat. It appears but a small leap to infer similar, albeit more complex, processes as applying to more complex species, such as man.

Uses in the Social Sciences

The concept of homeostasis has achieved widespread attention in the social sciences. Brown, for example, argues that homeostasis characterizes the stimulus-response-drive model in psychology and that territoriality and dominance have parallels in solidarity and status, which he sees as the fundamental dimensions of human social relationship. Equilibrium models have played a key role in economic theory since Adam Smith. We have already considered Leibenstein's (1957) characterization of backward economies as "quasi-stable equilibrium systems." In the following three sections, we shall limit our discussion to the use of equilibrium concepts in functionalism and systems theory, in cultural lag theory, and in human ecology theory.

Functionalism and Systems Theory

It has been persuasively argued that functionalism is at root an equilibrium theory. Kingsley Davis (1949: 634), for example, writes that "it is only in terms of equilibrium that most sociological concepts make sense. Either tacitly or explicitly, anyone who thinks about society tends to use the notion. The functional-structural approach to sociological analysis is basically an equilibrium theory." It has also been argued that equilibrium theory has a conservative bias against endogenous structural change. In the following discussion, several writings of Talcott Parsons will be explored, with emphasis given to equilibrium aspects and their alleged conservative bias. Parsons is selected because his works include arguments in favor of functionalism and elaborate the functionalist approach in a general systems theory.

In very general terms, Parsons (1964: 84) regards the "concept of stability . . . as a defining characteristic of structure . . . equivalent to the more specific concept of stable equilibrium—which in another reference may be either 'static' or 'moving.' " Structures are located in larger systems, however, and

> A system then is stable or (relatively) in equilibrium when the relation between its structure and the processes which go on within it and between its environment are such as to maintain those properties and relations, which for the purposes in hand have been called its structure, relatively unchanged. Very generally, always in "dynamic" systems, this maintenance is dependent on continuously varying processes, which "neutralize" either endogenous or exogenous sources of variability which, if they went far enough, would change the structure. . . .
> Contrasted then with stability or equilibrating processes are those processes which operate to bring about structural change. That such processes exist and that they are of fundamental scientific importance is nowhere in question (84).

Thus, Parsons distinguishes between those processes productive of structural stability and those productive of structural change.

> As I see it now, the distinction between the two pairs of concepts is one of system reference. The structure of a system and its environment must be distinguished from process *within* the system and in *interchange* between the system and its environment. But processes which maintain the stability of a system, internally both through structure and process, and in interchange between the system and its environment, *i.e.*, states of its equilibrium, must be distinguished from processes by which this balance between structure and more "elementary" processes is altered in such a way as to lead to a new and different "state" of the system, a state which must be described in terms of an alteration of its previous structure (85).

In theory at least, Parsons recognizes that structures change—that a condition of homeostasis obtains only for a limited set of system processes and system interchanges with environment. Indeed, at this level, Parsons seems excessively preoccupied with the possibility of change. A society consists of specialized systems and their subsystems, each engaged in a series of boundary exchanges with the other and with other "environments" external to the social system itself (i.e., the cultural system, or the personality system). All of these exchanges pose problems for the system, "forcing" the system to specialize in one or another of the four functional prerequisites for existence—adaptation, goal attainment, integration, and latent pattern maintenance.[2] Even the normative patterns that regulate the boundary interchanges are recognized to be potentially unstable:

> What, then, do we mean by the stability of an institutional complex? First, of course, is meant the stability of the normative pattern itself. . . . Second, stability implies a minimum level of commitment of acting units, *i.e.*, of dispositions to perform in accordance with the relevant expectations—rather than to evade or violate them. . . . Third, institutionalization implies acceptance of an empirical and mutually understood "definition of the situation" in a sense of understanding what the system of reference *is;* this can for example be ideologically distorted so as to make functioning impossible (1964: 87).

Perhaps this seeming preoccupation with the possibility of change provides us with a clue as to why functional analysis is charged with being excessively preoccupied with sources of stability. It seems that Parsons is so struck by the complexity of the social system, by the numerous things that must "hang together" if it is to work at all, that he has focused his attention almost exclusively on those aspects

[2] Technically speaking, all systems specialize in all four functions, through their subsystems—which in turn specialize in all four functions, through *their* subsystems (of each subsystem), and so forth.

of the social system that are functional, productive of
stability. Parsons (1954: 217) writes that the crucial role
of the concept of function

> . . . is to provide criteria of the *importance* of
> dynamic factors and processes within the system.
> They are important insofar as they have func-
> tional significance to the system, and their specific
> importance is understood in terms of the analysis
> of specific functional relations between the parts
> of the system and between it and its environment.
>   The significance of the concept of function
> implies the conception of the empirical system as
> a "going concern." Its structure is that system of
> determinate patterns which empirical observation
> shows, within certain limits, "tend to be main-
> tained" or on a somewhat more dynamic version
> "tend to develop" according to an empirically con-
> stant pattern (e.g., the pattern of growth of a
> young organism).
>   Functional significance in this context is in-
> herently teleological.

In conceiving of function in this sense, Parsons assures
that his focus will be on those system characteristics productive of stability or gradual (evolutionary) change. Thus,
Parsons has come to conceive of social systems and their
subsystems as existing in a cybernetic hierarchy, with
"conditions" at one end and "controls" at the other. Conditions provide the "givens" within which change must
occur; they relate ultimately to physical-organic environment. Controls govern change itself. They refer to "ultimate
reality" concepts and relate directly to cultural systems.
Moving from conditions to controls, one encounters systems
successively specialized in adaptation (the function closest
to the physical-organic environment), goal attainment, integration, and pattern maintenance (the function closest to
concerns with "ultimate reality"). At the action system
level, this means that the behavioral organism is highest
in the conditions hierarchy and lowest in the controls hierarchy; the cultural system is highest in controls and lowest
in conditions; and the social and personality systems occupy intermediate positions. At the social system level, this

society in the course of its history can and does change its structural type without any breach of continuity."

Cultural Lag Theory

Cultural lag theory is associated with William F. Ogburn. For present purposes, the important point is that cultural lag theory is merely a special form of general equilibrium theory.[5] It argues that societies operate as homeostatic mechanisms in that changes that upset equilibrium in one part tend to produce compensating changes to restore that equilibrium. In this case, however, the new equilibrium situation differs from the old (equilibrium can be said to be "moving"), and there is a lag between the two equilibrium states. "A cultural lag occurs when one of two parts of culture which are correlated changes before or in greater degree than the other part does, thereby causing less adjustment between the two parts than existed previously" (Ogburn, 1964: 86). While magnitude of maladjustment is presumably the critical variable, Ogburn, in his empirical references, appears to treat the length of the lag as a major operational indicator. Thus, in discussing workmen's compensation as a consequence of maladjustment between technological shifts (c. 1870) and the failure of the law to deal with these shifts, Ogburn (90) notes that "there was a lag of about thirty or forty years" between the shift and adoption of employer's liability and compensation in the United States (c. 1910). Societies tend to be in structural balance; when this balance is upset by changes in one part of a culture, compensating changes will occur in the other parts to reestablish balance. Ogburn (89) calls for the following steps in assessing the nature of a cultural lag:

(1) the identification of at least two variables;
(2) the demonstration that these two variables

[5] With respect to nonmaterial culture. With respect to material culture—i.e., technology—cultural lag theory is closer to evolutionary theory in positing smooth, cumulative change in the direction of ever increasing complexity.

were in adjustment; (3) the demonstration by dates that one variable has changed while the other has not changed or that one has changed in greater degree than the other; and (4) that when one variable has changed earlier or in greater degree than the other, there is a less satisfactory adjustment than existed before.

He (91) recognizes that "the extent of the generalized applicability of the theory rests on how much interconnection exists among the parts of a culture. . . . To the extent that culture is like a machine with parts that fit, cultural lag is widespread." He concludes that it is indeed widespread. Ogburn distinguishes between material culture (most notably, inventions) and nonmaterial or adaptive culture (customs, beliefs, philosophies, laws, governments—in general, values, beliefs, and the socially patterned ways of interaction). Changes in nonmaterial culture lag behind changes in material culture. For example, ". . . lags accumulate because of the great rapidity and volume of technological change" (92). Inventions, he (92) observes, increase exponentially, since existing inventions constitute an ever-increasing cultural base upon which future inventions can build,[6] the rest of the culture adapts to these inventions only after a period of lag. Ogburn's well-known example is the lag between the conservationist movement and the wholesale destruction of forests, a process begun when timber was plentiful and population scarce. Cultural lag theory is clearly an offshoot of evolutionism, at least insofar as both posit some directionality in change. In both instances, change is cumulative. While evolutionism focused primarily on the increasing complexity of society necessitated by adaptation (at ever higher levels) to environment, Ogburn (1922: 57) interposes the dynamic of material cultural accumulation in a sort of geometrically increasing technological adaptation to environment: new inventions broaden the cultural base, begetting ever newer inventions, until ". . . there is a good deal of evidence to indicate that the accumulation or growth of culture reaches

[6] The annual number of patents constitutes empirical evidence for this assertion.

a stage where certain inventions if not inevitable are certainly to a high degree probable." Unlike evolutionary theorists, however, Ogburn emphasizes the problematic nature of equilibrium among the parts of society; in so doing, he bridges the evolutionists and contemporary functionalists, particularly systems theorists such as Parsons and Smelser. If nothing else, Ogburn goes beyond most other functionalists in making strain inherent in society and focusing on what he feels are universal sources of maladjustment in all societies (or, at least, all changing societies). Like other functionalists, however, he believes that maladjustments generally tend to iron themselves out—that there are powerful forces operating in social systems to reduce tension and restore an equilibrium state.[7]

Human Ecology Theory

Human ecologists share a common perspective with Steward (multilinear evolution) and Sahlins (specific evolution). Borrowing from the plant and animal ecologists, they attempted to show how human communities patterned themselves spatially to optimize the relationship between man and habitat. The classical ecologists argued that hu-

[7] Four other examples of lag theory might be mentioned. De-Tocqueville (1955) attributes one of the major causes of the French Revolution to the fact that the hereditary aristocracy maintained its privilege long after its responsibilities had been assumed by other groups; thus, burdens once tolerated by the masses of people had since become intolerable. Karl Mannheim (1952), elaborating on Dilthey's concept of "contemporaneity," has suggested that the "critical experiences" undergone by persons during their young adult years is of major significance in explaining their outlook, attitudes, and behavior throughout subsequent life. Thus, the *Zeitgeist* changes in a wave-life fashion, as one group—its "spirit" forged by critical experiences during youth—is replaced by a subsequent group. Two lags exist here: a lag between "critical experiences" and the ascendence (to positions of power and responsibility) of the generational group; and a lag between succeeding generations. Zeitlin (1968) has applied this model to Cuban factory workers. Heberle (1951), defining generations with Mannheim as "those individuals of approximately the same age who have shared, at the same age, certain politically relevant experiences," applies the "generational lag" hypothesis to the study of pro-Nazi movements in Schleswig-Holstein during the period 1918–1932.

man culture is built upon a biotic or subsocial base resembling in many ways the relationships among plants and animals in a habitat. The underlying assumptions of this position are several (Park, 1961) : (1) the biotic community (contrasted with the culture or society) consists of a territorially organized population, (2) the population is more or less completely rooted in the soil it occupies, (3) individual units live in a state of mutual interdependence in a symbiotic relationship. This community possesses a mechanism (competition) for regulating the numbers and preserving the balance between the competing "species" of which it is composed. The twin concepts of territoriality and dominance, designated by Wynne-Edwards as the key homeostatic mechanisms among animals, are present here in virtually pure form. The classical ecologists (Park, 1961) strongly insisted that the biotic level was distinct from the cultural or social level, that it alone constituted substructure and all else was superstructure, and that the "biotic level energies" were seen on higher social levels in more "subtle and sublimated forms." Competition (seen as a subsocial process) determines communal order through the processes of dominance and succession. One group competes with another, dominates it, and a climax (or maturity) is reached, until further changes result in renewed competition, new succession and dominance (McKenzie, 1961).[8] Overlaying the biotic substructure was the "cultural superstructure," made possible for man because of language. If the biotic level is characterized by subsocial competition, the cultural level is characterized by communication, custom, and consensus. "Society" restructures competition and thus promotes cooperation among its members. But, according to Park, no matter how much the biotic competition has declined and been replaced by societal cooperation, the struggle for existence remains at the basis of human relationships, emerging in more sublimated forms.

The classical position proved to be empirically untenable; indeed, it was impossible to abstract the biotic from

[8] McKenzie (1961) identified several basic ecological processes resulting from competition, including concentration, centralization, segregation, invasion, and succession.

the cultural in empirical research, and nearly so analytically. Thus, during the thirties and forties, the classical position eroded under the criticism of Alihan (1961), Hollingshead (1961), Quinn (1961), Hawley (1961), and others. The distinction between biotic and cultural levels, once seen as a defining characteristic of human ecology, was relaxed, and the study of spatial patterning, which had characterized most of ecological research, gave way partially to the study of community structure and organization.[9] The legacy of human ecology proved to be a methodology—a technique for studying the spatial distribution of populations according to their means of livelihood with concepts such as "zones," "natural areas," "social areas," "gradients," and "indices of dissimilarity." Underlying all of these concepts, however, is the concept we have identified as homeostasis: for any given habitat or configuration of conditions, populations will tend to distribute themselves in such a fashion that the final patterning will prove stable and resistant to further change. Through the struggle for dominance, group will succeed group until some "optimal" patterning is achieved that represents the climax, given the territorial conditions and the nature of the populations. Further change must come from inputs exogenous to the mature ecological community. Although such changes could originate at the level of society (e.g., by way of new inventions—either technological, social, or organizational), in practice, many ecologists apparently felt they must originate totally outside the population. Thus, Burgess' (1961) zonal hypothesis holds that through a process of succession, each inner zone tends to extend its area by the invasion of the next outer zone in an unending process of succession and dominance. This, Burgess feels, is productive of social disorganization. But why does this process occur in metropolitan areas in an unending sequence? Primarily because of migration into the cities, seen as a prime cause of social disorganization. Succeeding waves of migrants feed the

[9] Hawley (1961) redefined the central concern of ecology in the following terms: "How does a population *organize* to maintain itself in a given area?" This redefinition provides the link between ecology and community studies.

inner zone of the city (the factory zone and the zone of transition), providing an exogenous source of continuous change. Thus, the homeostatic nature of the process is obscured through the introduction of external sources of change. In this the ecologists were true functionalists.

REFERENCES

Alihan, Milla A.
    1961   "Community and ecological studies." (1938) In George A. Theodorson (ed.), Studies in Human Ecology. New York: Harper & Row.
Brown, Roger.
    1965   Social Psychology. New York: Free Press.
Burgess, Ernest W.
    1961   "The growth of the city." (1925) In G. A. Theodorson (ed.), Studies in Human Ecology, New York: Row, Peterson.
Dahrendorf, Ralf.
    1959   Class and Class Conflict in Industrial Society. Stanford, Calif.: Stanford University Press.
Davis, Kingsley.
    1949   Human Society. New York: Macmillan.
DeTocqueville, Alexis.
    1955   The Old Regime and the French Revolution. New York: Doubleday.
Etzioni, Amitai, and Eva Etzioni, eds.
    1964   Social Change. New York: Basic Books.
Guessous, Mohammed.
    1967   "A general critique of equilibrium theory." In Wilbert E. Moore and Robert M. Cook (eds.), Readings on Social Change. Englewood Cliffs, N.J.: Prentice-Hall.
Hawley, Amos H.
    1961   "Discussion of Hollingshead's 'Community Research: Development and Present Condition.'" (1948) In George A. Theodorson (ed.), Studies in Human Ecology. New York: Harper & Row.
Heberle, Rudolph.

1951 Social Movements: An Introduction to Political Sociology. New York: Appleton-Century-Crofts.

Hollingshead, August B.
1961 "A re-examination of ecological theory." (1947) In George A. Theodorson (ed.), Studies in Human Ecology. New York: Harper & Row.

Homans, George C.
1950 The Human Group. New York: Harcourt, Brace & World.

Leibenstein, Harvey.
1957 Economic Backwardness and Economic Growth. Cambridge: University Press.

Mannheim, Karl.
1952 Essays in the Sociology of Knowledge. Edited by Paul Kecskemeti. New York: Oxford University Press.

Moore, Wilbert E., and Robert M. Cook, eds.
1967 Readings on Social Change. Englewood Cliffs, N.J.: Prentice-Hall.

Moore, Wilbert E., and Arnold S. Feldman, eds.
1962 Transactions of the Fifth World Congress of Sociology. Vol. 2. Louvain, Belgium: International Sociological Association.

Ogburn, William F.
1922 Social Change: With Respect to Culture and Original Nature. New York: B. W. Heubsch.
1964 On Culture and Social Change. Chicago: University of Chicago Press.

Park, Robert E.
1961 "Human ecology." (1936) In George A. Theodorson (ed.), Studies in Human Ecology. New York: Harper & Row.

Parsons, Talcott.
1951 The Social System. New York: Free Press.
1954 Essays in Sociological Theory. Rev. ed. New York: Free Press.
1960 Structure and Process in Modern Societies. New York: Free Press.
1964 "A functional theory of change." In Amitai and

Eva Etzioni (eds.), Social Change. New York: Basic Books.
1966   Societies: Evolutionary and Comparative Perspectives. Englewood Cliffs, N.J.: Prentice-Hall.
Zeitlin, Maurice.
1968   "Political generations in the Cuban working class." In James Petras and Maurice Zeitlin, Latin America: Reform or Revolution? Greenwich, Conn.: Fawcett.
Quinn, James A.
1961   "The nature of human ecology." (1939) In George A. Theodorson (ed.), Studies in Human Ecology. New York: Harper & Row.
Radcliffe-Brown, Alfred R.
1952   Structure and Function in Primitive Society. London: Cohen and West.
Theodorson, George A., ed.
1961   Studies in Human Ecology. New York: Harper & Row.
Wynne-Edwards, V. C.
1962   Animal Dispersions in Relation to Social Behavior. Edinburgh; London: Oliver & Boyd.

3

Conflict Theory: Change as Endemic to All Social Organisms

All theories that have thus far been examined conceive of society as an organism characterized by a fair degree of stability. The parts are postulated to "hang together" in a system of functional interdependence, much like a human body or a relatively smooth-running machine. Different theorists have different positions regarding change (all claim to be theories of social change), but change is seldom conceived of as altering the fundamental structure of society. Another class of theories, however, focuses on change itself, regarding change as inherent in all social organisms. It is important to note that all three classes of theory thus far considered are organismic; all conceive of society as a set of mutually interdependent structures that operate in a functional (or dysfunctional) fashion for one another. But if evolutionary and equilibrium theories see stability everywhere, conflict theories see structural change everywhere. Conflict theories constitute the legacy of Karl Marx, whom we shall consider first.

Marxism: The Dialectics of Change

Dahrendorf (1959: 28) has written that

> For Marx, society is not primarily a smoothly functioning order of the form of a social organism, a social system, or a static social fabric. Its dominant characteristic is, rather, the continuous change of not only its elements, but its very structural form. This change in turn bears witness to the presence of conflicts as an essential feature of every society. Conflicts are not random; they are a systematic product of the structure of society itself. According to this image, there is no order except in the regularity of change.

Or, in Marx's (1959: 27) words, "Without conflict no progress: this is the law which civilization has followed to the present day." More specifically, "The history of all societies up to the present is the history of class struggles." (From "Manifesto of the Communist Party," in Feuer, 1959: 7). For Marx, the key to understanding structure and conflict in any period lies in the mode of production, i.e., the state of technology, for this determines the relations of production (the organization of production), and together they constitute the substructure of society. Everything else, social institutions, values and beliefs, is superstructure.

> According to the materialist conception of history, the *ultimately* determining element in history is the production and reproduction of real life. More than this neither Marx nor I has ever asserted. Hence if somebody twists this into saying that the economic element is the *only* determining one he transforms that proposition into a meaningless, abstract, senseless phrase. The economic situation is the basis, but the various elements of the superstructure—political forms of the class struggle and its results, to wit: constitutions established by the victorious class after a successful battle, etc., juridical forms, and even the reflexes of all these actual struggles in the brains of the participants, political, juristic, philosophical theories, religious views, and their fur-

ther development into systems of dogmas—also exercise their influence upon the course of the historical struggles and in many cases preponderate in determining their *form*. There is an interaction of all these elements in which, amidst all the endless host of accidents (that is, of things and events whose inner interconnection is so remote or so impossible of proof that we can regard it as nonexistent, as negligible), the economic movement finally asserts itself as necessary (from a letter from F. Engels to J. Bloch (1890), Feuer, 1958: 397–398).

Society is a system, in that all of these elements hang together in a determinate way. But for Marx, if not for systems theorists, that way is inherently unstable in the long run. Marx offers several postulates regarding the development of class structure: (1) In a capitalistic society, classes tend to polarize increasingly: society breaks up into two hostile classes, the bourgeoisie and the proletariat. (2) As the classes polarize, their situations become increasingly extreme, with sections of the proletariat becoming increasingly pauperized and with society's wealth increasingly concentrated in the hands of a relative few.[1] (3) As the classes polarize, they become more homogeneous internally, with other groupings absorbed into the two classes. (4) Once these processes reach their extreme, revolution terminates the existing arrangement and a new society emerges, with the formerly oppressed class in power. This is true at all stages of class history save the last: the proletarian revolution ultimately results in a classless society, since the proletariat is the last historical class. This latter point rests on an assumption important for Marx—that the

[1] Mandel (1968: vol. 1, 151) notes that "The idea that the real wages of the workers tend to decline more and more is totally alien to Marx's writings. . . . Actually, he always insisted on the fact that wages are determined by complex laws and that denunciation of the capitalist order must be independent of the relative level of wages. What one finds in Marx is an idea of the absolute impoverishment not of the workers, the wage-earners, but of that section of the proletariat which the capitalist system *throws out* of the production process: unemployed, old people, disabled persons, cripples, the sick, etc., *die Lazarusschicht des Proletariats* as he calls it, the poorest stratum 'bearing the stigmata of wage labour'."

functional indispensibility of a class in the economic system leads to its political supremacy in the society as a whole.

Thus, conflict and change reflect the distribution of power in society. Stinchcombe (1968: 93–94) summarizes the Marxian postulates concerning power as follows:

> (1) The relative power of social classes is determined by the mode of production, by the authority system required by a given technology, and by who owns the productive property. (2) The mode of production changes over time with advancing technology, extension of the market, larger units of production, and the like. (3) Hence the distribution of power among classes changes systematically over historical time.
>
> The reason changing power distributions cause changes in institutions ("superstructure") is that *the greater the power of a class, the more effective that class is as a cause of social structures.*

Structural change occurs, therefore, as the proletariat acquires power at the expense of the bourgeoisie and other class remnants disappear or align themselves with one of the two major classes. To the extent that the bourgeoisie rules the state, a "lag" from the earlier period when the bourgeoisie itself was the most functionally indispensible (and hence powerful) class, the state must employ increasing coercion to keep the proletariat from assuming political power. This creates tension, particularly in light of the increasing polarization of the classes and pauperization of segments of the working class. "The main source of tension is clearly the support of other classes for structures which harm a given class" (98). The processes by which revolutionary class consciousness arises, by which classes of themselves become classes for themselves, need not detain us, except to note that classes are forged only out of struggle. "Individuals form a class only insofar as they are engaged in a common struggle with another class" (Marx and Engels, The German Ideology, in Feuer, 1959a: 14). The immediate conditions giving rise to class consciousness, such as the development of railroads permitting increased communications among class members and the concentration of workers in factories, can be considered to be structurally conducive to the development of class consciousness. The ultimate determinant, however, is the struggle between those who control the means of production and those workers who actually perform the productive function.

Thus, instability inheres in social structure since there is always tension between the forces and the mode of production. The process of change is dialectical in that "the two classes stand in the relation of Hegel's 'thesis' and 'antithesis,' in the sense that one is characterized by the affirmation (or possession) of those features of which the other is the complete negation" (20). Furthermore, the historical sequence of change is itself dialectical in that in any given epoch, the dominant class carries within itself the seeds of its own future destruction in the form of a class which it creates to provide the productive forces necessary for its own existence. Thus, following the demise of feudalism, the bourgeoisie emerged as the dominant class. But

> . . . the essential condition for the existence, and for the sway of the bourgeois class, is the formation and augmentation of capital; the condition for capital is wage labor. Wage labor rests exclusively on competition between the laborers. The advance of industry, whose involuntary promoter is the bourgeoisie, replaces the isolation of the laborers, due to competition, by their revolutionary combination, due to association. The development of modern industry, therefore, cuts from under its feet the very foundation on which the bourgeoisie produces and appropriates products. What the bourgeoisie produces, above all, is its own grave-diggers. Its fall and the victory of the proletariat are equally inevitable. (Marx and Engels, "Manifesto to the Communist Party," in Feuer, 1959: 18).

If the bourgeoisie and proletariat stand in the relation of thesis and antithesis, so do capitalist society and the dictatorship of the proletariat. And, ultimately, the clash of thesis and antithesis gives rise to the new synthesis—in this case, to the classless society with no political authority.

> The condition of the liberation of the working class is the abolition of every class, just as the condition of the liberation of the Third Estate, i.e., the establishment of the bourgeois order, was the abolition of all estates.
>
> The working class will in the course of development replace the old bourgeois society by an association which excludes classes and their conflict, and there will no longer be any political authority proper, since it is especially the political authority that provides class conflict within bourgeois society with its official expression. . . .
>
> Only in an order of things in which there are no classes and no class conflict will all social evolutions cease to be political revolutions (Marx and Engels, 1959 : 18).

The kernel of the Marxist argument regarding social change is contained in this last statement.

Although we have focused attention primarily on the nature of social change and the class struggle in what Marx identified as the last phase of that struggle, the downfall of capitalism, Marx applied his dialectical materialism to the whole of history. He thus identified the tension arising from the relations of production through the tribal, communal, and feudal periods, as well as the capitalist and communist periods.

> The production of life, both of one's own in labor and of fresh life in procreation, now appears as a double relationship: on the one hand as a natural, on the other as a social relationship. By social we understand the cooperation of several individuals, no matter under what conditions, in what manner, and to what end. It follows from this that a certain mode of production or industrial stage is always combined with a certain mode of co-operation, or social stage, and this mode of cooperation is itself a "productive force." Further, that the multitude of productive forces accessible to men determines the nature of society (Marx and Engels, The German Ideology,

in Feuer, 1959: 251; see also Marx, 1967: Part VIII; Mandel, 1968).

According to Marx, the whole of history can be divided into three periods that stand in a dialectical relationship. At the beginning of history, man is free, "with himself." But his freedom is incomplete: man is chained to nature, a slave to it, and although the division of labor, classes, and class conflict are absent, man's freedom is dull and purposeless. This period (thesis) is replaced by another (its antithesis) which constitutes the whole of known history to the present. During the second period, man develops technology and exercises increasing control over nature. But in doing so, he becomes alienated because the essential mechanism for this control is the division of labor, which means alienated labor.

> With the division of labor . . . is given simultaneously the distribution, and indeed the unequal distribution (both quantitative and qualitative), of labor and its products, hence property: the nucleus, the first form, of which lies in the family, where wife and children are the slaves of the husband. This latent slavery in the family, though still very crude, is the first property, but even at this early stage it corresponds perfectly to the definition of modern economists who call it the power of disposing of the labor power of others. Division of labor and private property are, moreover, identical expressions. . . .
> Further, the division of labor implies the contradiction between the interest of the separate individual or the individual family and the communal interest of all individuals who have intercourse with one another. . . . And finally, the division of labor offers us the first example of how, as long as man remains in natural society— that is, as long as a cleavage exists between the particular and the common interest—as long, therefore, as activity is not voluntarily but naturally divided, man's own deed becomes an alien power opposed to him, which enslaves him instead of being controlled by him. For as soon as labor is distributed, each man has a particular, exclusive sphere of activity which is forced upon

him and from which he cannot excape (Marx
and Engels, The German Ideology, in Feuer,
1959: 253–254).

Thus, whereas man is fast developing the means for
self-realization and freedom, he is becoming increasingly
enchained. "Division of labor and private property create
relations of domination and subjection, class formations,
and class struggles in ever-changing patterns. Indeed, private property is the specific difference of this second stage
of the historical process (Dahrendorf, 1959: 29)." The
talents and potentialities developed by man during this
stage cry out for freedom and realization; man comes to
seek an end to his alienated state.

This "estrangement" (to use a term which
will be comprehensible to the philosophers) can,
of course, be abolished given only two *practical*
premises. For it to become an "intolerable"
power, i.e., a power against which men make a
revolution, it must necessarily have rendered the
great mass of humanity "propertyless" and produced, at the same time, the contradiction of an
existing world of wealth and culture, both of
which conditions presuppose a great increase in
productive power, a high degree of its development. And, on the other hand, this development
of productive forces (which itself implies the
actual empirical existence of men in their *world-
historical,* instead of local, being) is absolutely
necessary as a practical premise: first, for the
reason that without it only *want* is made general,
and with want the struggle for necessities and all
the old filthy business would necessarily be re-
produced; and second, because only with this universal development of productive forces is a *universal* intercourse between men established which
produces in all nations simultaneously the phe-
nomenon of the "propertyless" mass (universal
competition), makes each nation dependent on the
revolutions of the others, and finally has put
world-historical, empirically universal individuals
in place of local ones (Marx and Engels, The German Ideology, in Feuer, 1959: 256).

And so emerges the third period (synthesis), the classless society. Private property has been abolished and, since private property is the basis for all conflict and struggle, classes, class conflict, the division of labor, and the need for political authority have also disappeared.

> . . . in communist society, where nobody has one exclusive sphere of activity but each can become accomplished in any branch he wishes, society regulates the general production and thus makes it possible for me to do one thing today and another tomorrow, to hunt in the morning, fish in the afternoon, rear cattle in the evening, criticize after dinner, just as I have a mind, without ever becoming hunter, fisherman, shepherd, or critic (254).[2]

The third period "is a synthesis, because it combines the dull liberty of original society and the differentiated human potentialities of alienation [that characterized the second great stage of history] . . . it abolishes them as such and yet preserves them on a higher level. In this society man realizes himself as a free being" (Dahrendorf, 1959: 29). Thus, the young Marx sees the final state as a return to the earliest period: the vision of society as an organism, ever increasing in complexity, is replaced with one of an undifferentiated unity, free from class, conflict, and authority. The resemblance between Marx and the evolutionary or equilibrium theorists has vanished with this final philosophical leap.

Marx's writings were largely concerned with the origins and nature of west European capitalism, and his empirical evidence came from the European, and primarily British, context. At the time of the writing of *Capital* (the first German edition of volume 1 was published in 1867), European colonization had not yet begun in earnest, although settlement of sparsely populated areas in America and

---

[2] *The German Ideology* was written when Marx and Engels were in their mid-twenties. Feuer (1959: 246) notes that "Marx and Engels, in their early period, held an exaggerated expectation that the division of labor would end under 'Communism.'"

Australia did focus Marx's attention on the failure of capitalists to successfully expropriate the propertied settlers in these areas.[3] From the 1880's until the outbreak of World War I, however, a final spurt of European imperialism secured its domination over the rest of the world—the direct control of Africa and Pacific island areas, and the economic control of much of Asia and the Near East. European imperialism received a Marxist analysis at the hands of Lenin, in a pamphlet entitled *Imperialism, the Highest Stage of Capitalism.*

Lenin does not define imperialism as the term is customarily used; that is, the domination of vast territories by force and the subsequent economic exploitation of their populations and resources. Rather, he (1966: 213) defines imperialism as "the rule of finance capital," the highest stage of capitalism, in which the separation of the ownership of capital (the *rentier*) from the productive application of capital (the entrepreneur) ". . . reaches vast proportions. The supremacy of finance capital over all other forms of capital means the rule of the *rentier* and of the financial oligarchy; it means the crystallization of a small number of financially powerful states from among all the rest" (213). Lenin traces the historical development of monopoly capital, the rapid concentration of capital in the hands of a few monopoly combines that first divided the markets of their home countries and then, through the export of capital and the formation of international cartels, divided control over world markets. "The non-economic

[3] For example, in *Capital*, Chapter 33, entitled "The Modern Theory of Colonization," Marx (1967: 768) notes that "We have seen that the expropriation of the mass of the people from the soil forms the basis of the capitalist mode of production. The essence of a free colony, on the contrary, consists in this—that the bulk of the soil is still public property, and every settler on it therefore can turn part of it into his private property and individual means of production, without hindering the later settlers in the same operation. This is the secret both of the prosperity of the colonies and of their inveterate vice—opposition to the establishment of capital. Where land is very cheap and all men are free, where every one who so pleases can easily obtain a piece of land for himself, not only is labour very dear, as respects the labourer's share of the produce, but the difficulty is to obtain combined labour at any price."

superstructure which grows up on the basis of finance capital, its politics and its ideology, stimulates the striving for colonial conquest" (234). Imperialism, then, can be briefly defined as "the monopoly stage of capitalism" (237).

> Such a definition would include what is most important, for, on the one hand, finance capital is the bank capital of the few big monopolist banks, merged with the capital of the monopolist combines of manufacturers; and, on the other hand, the division of the world is the transition from a colonial policy which has extended without hindrance to territories unoccupied by any capitalist power, to a colonial policy of the monopolistic possession of the territories of the world which have been completely divided up (237).

Imperialism is seen by Lenin (237) as having five essential features:

> (1) The concentration of production and capital developed to such a stage that it creates monopolies which play a decisive role in economic life.
>
> (2) The merging of bank capital with industrial capital, and the creation, on the basis of "finance capital," of a financial oligarchy.
>
> (3) The export of capital, which has become extremely important, as distinguished from the export of commodities.
>
> (4) The formation of international capitalist monopolies which share the world among themselves.
>
> (5) The territorial division of the world as a whole among the greatest capitalist powers is completed.

Lenin felt that the stage of imperialism followed inevitably from the development of capitalism in the direction of monopolistic concentration of capital (predicted by Marx) and the ever-expanding demand for raw materials and markets that results. Once the exportation of capital has reached large proportions, stagnation sets in. "Like all monopoly, this capitalist monopoly inevitably gives rise to a tendency to stagnation and decay. . . . The export of capital, one of the essential economic bases of imperialism, still more completely isolates the *rentiers* from production and sets the seal of parasitism on the whole country that lives by the exploitation of the labor of several overseas countries and colonies" (246). The *rentiers* amass the wealth from their capital, with cheap labor performed in the colonial nations. Capital is diverted from domestic investment (where labor is relatively expensive) to foreign (colonial) investment, where cheap labor promises higher returns. This promotes stagnation in the mother country, intensifying the division between worker and capitalist. Imperialism is thus "moribund capitalism" (268) ; it intensifies the contradictions of capitalism, and marks the final stage before the proletarian revolution :

> The extent to which monopolist capital has intensified all the contradictions of capitalism is generally known. It is sufficient to mention the high cost of living and the power of the trusts. This intensification of contradictions constitutes the most powerful driving force of the transitional period of history, which began at the time of the definite victory of world finance capital.
> Monopolies, oligarchy, the striving for domination instead of the striving for liberty, the exploitation of an increasing number of small or weak nations by an extremely small group of the richest or most powerful nations—all these have given birth to those distinctive features of imperialism which compel us to define it as parasitic or decaying capitalism (266–267).

The Marxist vision, modified somewhat to take into account the historical exploitation of African or Asian labor as well as German, English or Russian labor, applies to Lenin's position. But if this colonial exploitation has postponed the eventual revolutionary demise of capitalism, its ultimate fate is unchanged.

Marx has been criticized on a number of grounds, with most criticism calling attention to empirical weaknesses in his theory. Thus, capitalist societies historically have failed to polarize into two increasingly opposed camps; rather, innumerable differentiations have occurred, resulting in continuous gradations of groups rather than polar opposites. Both the capitalist and working class have decomposed and become increasingly heterogeneous. It is also argued that the increasing impoverishment of workers and aggrandizement of wealth in the hands of capitalists has not occurred; allegedly, the distribution of wealth has equalized. Marx also failed to foresee the separation of ownership, control, and technical expertise in the operation of capitalist ventures, and he did not accurately assess the effects of increasing social mobility. Dahrendorf criticizes Marx for limiting the resolution of class conflict to violent upheaval. This, Dahrendorf (1959: 131) implies, represents an essentially static view of social structures.[4] Other critics have questioned Marx's treatment of class as one-dimensional (related only to the possession of property) and his disregard of increasing bureaucracy. From a sociological point of view, however, Marx can be criticized on two principal grounds: his view of society as inherently conflict generating rather than conflict reducing (and hence, his class analysis), and the introduction of essentially metaphysical concepts (such as the classless society) into the theory. The first criticism need only be noted. There is, at present, no adequate criteria in the social sciences by which evolutionary or equilibrium theories and conflict theories, in their present forms, can be compared and assessed relative to one another in terms of overall explanatory power.[5] The second criticism is taken up by Dahrendorf, and is considered below.

Modern Conflict Theory: The Marxist Metaphysics Rejected, Notions of Conflict Retained

Conflict theory virtually died in American and English sociology during the twentieth century. With the exception of such men as Webbs and Sumner, and aspects of the writings of Simmel, Small, Vold, and a few others, Amer-

[4] Dahrendorf (1959: 131) sees Marx and Parsons as "meeting here in a curious fashion: both of them freeze the flow of the historical process in the idea of a 'system.' "

[5] See Chapter 5, below.

ican sociologists neglected conflict theory, and it was eventually defined outside the mainstream of American sociology (see, for example, Parsons, 1937). Recently, however, there has been a revival of the conflict focus in the writings of Dahrendorf (1959, 1964), Aron (1954), Brinton (1952), Kerr (1954), Coser (1956), and others. We shall consider only the work of Dahrendorf (1964: 100), who states:

> The intent of a sociological theory of conflict is to overcome the predominantly arbitrary nature of unexplained historical events by deriving these events from elements of their social structures, in other words, to explain certain processes by prognostic connections. . . . Thus it is the task of sociology to derive conflicts from specific social structures, and not to relegate these conflicts to psychological variables ("aggressiveness") or to descriptive-historical ones (the influx of Negroes into the United States) or to chance.

Dahrendorf (103) identifies the underlying assumptions of what he terms structural-functional theory as fourfold:

(1) Every society is a relatively persisting configuration of elements.
(2) Every society is a well integrated configuration of elements.
(3) Every element in a society contributes to its functioning.
(4) Every society rests on the consensus of its members.

Contrasted with this is the conflict model, which takes the opposite position on each of these assumptions:

(1) Every society is subjected at every moment to change; social change is ubiquitous.
(2) Every society experiences at every moment social conflict; social conflict is ubiquitous.
(3) Every element in a society contributes to its change.
(4) Every society rests on constraint of some of its members by others (103).

A conflict theory will thus enable the social scientist to "derive social conflicts from structural arrangements and thus show these conflicts systematically generated;" it will further "account for both the multiplicity of forms of conflict and for their degrees of intensity." Finally, it will answer the following questions:

(1) How do conflicting groups arise from the structure of society?
(2) What forms can the struggles among such groups assume?
(3) How does the conflict among such groups effect a change in the social structures? (all quotes from Dahrendorf, 1964: 105).

Dahrendorf (1959: 27–32) explicitly rejects what he terms the "philosophical elements of Marx's theory of class" —the Marxist metaphysics. Philosophical elements are those not subject to empirical proof or refutation. "Propositions such as that capitalist society is the last class society of history, or that communist society leads to complete realization of human freedom, can be disputed and denied, but they cannot be refuted with the tools of science" (28). Marx's philosophy of history is thus the principal metaphysical element in his theory and is tied in with his sociology of class conflict by virtue of the historical convergence of three conditions: the presence of group (class) conflict, effective private property, and authority relations (of domination and subjugation). "By asserting the dependence of classes on relations of domination and subjection, and the dependence of these relations on the possession of or exclusion from effective private capital, he makes on the one hand empirically private property, on the other hand philosophically social classes, the central factor of his analyses" (30). This is both the strength and weakness of Marxist theory, for, as Dahrendorf (30–31) notes, "had Marx, conversely, defined private property by authority relations [rather than asserting the dependence of authority relations on private property], his empirical observation [the disappearance of private property] would not have 'fitted,' and he would have had to drop his philosophy of history.

For effective private property many disappear entirely, but authority relations can do so only by the magic trick of the system maniac."

What Dahrendorf accepts from Marx is the heuristic aspect of class as the most useful device in explaining conflict. But, avoiding the pitfall he perceives in Marxist theory, Dahrendorf redefines class in terms of authority relations (rather than, with Marx, in terms of property relations). From this redefinition, Dahrendorf's theory of class conflict follows. In its major elements, that theory can be summarized as follows:

> 1. In every imperatively coordinated group, the carriers of positive and negative dominance roles determine two quasigroups with opposite latent interests. We call them "quasigroups" because we have to do here with mere aggregates, not organized units: we speak of "latent interests," because the opposition of outlook may not be conscious on this level; it may exist only in the form of expectations associated with certain positions. The opposition of interests has here quite a formal meaning, namely, the expectation that an interest in the preservation of the status quo is associated with the positive dominance roles and an interest in the change of the status quo is associated with the negative dominance roles. 2. The bearers of positive and negative dominance roles, that is, the members of the opposing quasigroups, organize themselves into groups with manifest interests, unless certain empirically variable conditions (the condition of organization) intervene. Interest groups, in contrast to quasigroups, are organized entities, such as parties and trade unions; the manifest interests are formulated programs and ideologies. 3. Interest groups which originate in this manner are in constant conflict over the preservation or change of the status quo. The form and intensity of the conflict are determined by empirically variable conditions (the conditions of conflict). 4. The conflict among interest groups in this sense of the model leads to changes in the structure of their social relations, through changes in the dominance relations. The kind, the speed, and the depth of this development

depend on empirically variable conditions (the conditions of structural change) (1964: 107).[6]

Dahrendorf has thus distilled from Marxism those elements necessary to formulate a theory of interest group conflict, and nothing more. This is wholly in keeping with his conception of Marx's theory of class, which Dahrendorf (1959: 26) sees as "a theory of structural change by revolutions based on conflicts between antagonistic interest groups." Dahrendorf's theory is thus not a theory of societal change but a general theory of social (group) conflict. Having lost the grandiose sweep of Marxism along with what Dahrendorf regards as its philosophical elements, it is doubtful that Dahrendorf's version of conflict theory will replace the Marxist theory of societal change in the eyes of many people. Whether Dahrendorf's theory will prove fruitful in the more limited analysis of interest group conflict and structural change remains to be demonstrated.

REFERENCES

Aron, Raymond.
1966   "Social structure and the ruling class." In Reinhard Bendix and Seymour Lipset (eds), Class, Status, and Power: A Reader in Social Stratification. New York: Free Press.
Bendix, Reinhard, and Seymour Lipset, eds.
1966   Class, Status, and Power: A Reader in Social Stratification. New York: Free Press.
Brinton, Crane.
1952   The Anatomy of a Revolution. New York: Knopf.
Christman, H. M.
1966   The Essential Works of Lenin. New York: Bantam Books.
Coser, Lewis.
1956   The Functions of Social Conflict. Glencoe, Ill.: Free Press.
Dahrendorf, Ralf.

[6] For a more elaborate yet concise summary in propositional form, see Dahrendorf (1959: 237–240).

1959   Class and Class Conflict in Industrial Society.
        Stanford, Calif.: Stanford University Press.
1964   "Towards a theory of social conflict." Reprinted
        in Amitai and Eva Etzioni (eds.), Social Change.
        New York: Basic Books.
Etzioni, Amitai, and Eva Etzioni, eds.
1964   Social Change. New York: Basic Books.
Feuer, Lewis S., ed.
1959   Marx and Engels, Basic Writings on Politics and
        Philosophy. New York: Doubleday.
Kerr, Clark.
1954   "Industrial conflict and its mediation." American
        Journal of Sociology 40.
Lenin, Vladimir I.
1966   The Essential Works of Lenin. H. M. Christman
        (ed.). New York: Bantam Books.
Mandel, Ernest.
1968   Marxist Economic Theory. Vol 1. London: Merlin
        Press.
Marx, Karl.
1967   Capital. Vol. 1, The Process of Capitalist Produc-
        tion. New York: International Publishers.
Marx, Karl, and Friedrich Engels.
1959   Das Elend der Philosophie. As quoted and trans-
        lated in Ralf Dahrendorf, Class and Class Conflict
        in Industrial Society. Stanford, Calif.: Stanford
        University Press.
Parsons, Talcott.
1937   The Structure of Social Action. New York: Mc-
        Graw-Hill.
Stinchcombe, Arthur L.
1968   Constructing Social Theories. New York: Har-
        court, Brace & World.

4
Rise and Fall Theories: Processes of Growth and Decay

The final class of theories we will consider regards societies (or, more generally, civilizations) as experiencing periods of growth and decline, often drawing analogies with the human organism. Rise and fall theories differ from other classes of theories, which viewed change as cumulative and in the uniform direction of increasing complexity. We shall briefly review three of the theories of this class.

Spengler (1964: 21) states that "cultures are organisms, and world history is their collective biography."

> Every culture passes through the age-phases of the individual man. Each has its childhood, youth, manhood, and old age. It is a young and trembling soul, heavy with misgivings, that reveals itself in the morning of Romanesque and Gothic. . . . Childhood speaks to us also—and in the same tones—out of early Homeric Doric, out of early Christian (which is really Arabian) arts. . . . The more nearly a culture approaches the noon culmination of its being, the more virile, austere, controlled, intense the form-language it has secured for itself, the more assured its sense of its

own power, the clearer its lineaments. . . . At last, in the gray dawn of civilization, the fire in the soul dies down. The dwindling powers rise to one more half-successful effort of creation and produce the classicism that is common to all dying cultures. The soul sinks once again and in Romanticism looks piteously back to its childhood; then finally, weary, reluctant, cold, it loses its desire to be and, as in imperial Rome, wishes itself out of the overlong daylight and back in the darkness of protomysticism, in the womb of the mother, in the grave (23–24). . . .

Spengler (24) asserts that the parallel between the life cycle of the culture and the human organism extends to the determinate, fixed length of generations as well: "Every culture, every adolescence and maturing and decay of a culture, every one of its intrinsically necessary stages and periods, have a definite duration, always the same, always recurring with the emphasis of a symbol. . . ." Thus, the period of "political, intellectual, and artistic 'becoming' " is said to last 50 years, the manhood of culture—its full flowering—300 years; the entire life cycle of a culture a millenium. Furthermore, all cultures are characterized by homology or morphological equivalence in that ". . . all great creations and forms in religion, art, politics, social life, economy, and science appear, fulfill themselves, and die down *contemporaneously* in all cultures; the inner structure of one corresponds strictly with that of all the others (26). . . ."

Spengler's methodology consists in drawing numerous examples from diverse cultural contexts, and thus amassing evidence for his assertions. He rejects the scientific search for causes that characterize "the methods of Darwinism;" his approach, like Comte's, is eminently holistic. If the parallels drawn between human and cultural life cycles have a certain fascination, this fascination lies more in the realm of art than of science (as Spengler would undoubtedly insist). Assuming the parallels to be 100 percent demonstrated, which they most clearly are not, they still explain nothing; a culture is not a human organism, and any coincidence between the life cycles of the two does not lie on the level of actual processes. Organismic theorists have addressed themselves to this point and have attempted to reconstruct the biological concepts they employ so as to render them directly applicable to the analysis of society (e.g., differentiation). Spengler is content merely to draw analogies.

Sorokin, like Spengler, sees history as his subject matter—for example, the art forms characteristic of different periods and cultures, as compiled in the *Encyclopedia Britannica* (discussion based on Sorokin, 1941; 1947). Sorokin seeks to establish regularities and patterns ("constellations of conditions") among seemingly unique historical events; in this he was strongly influenced by Spengler, Marx, and Toynbee. His focus is on "supersystems" which integrate the various cultural elements at any given time; these supersystems are based on the most

> general of all ontological principles, namely, *the one defining the ultimate nature of reality and value*. Ontologically there are no more all-embracing concepts than the three following definitions of the ultimate nature of reality and value: (a) True reality and true value are sensory—the major premise of the sensate supersystems. (b) True value and true reality consist in a supersensory, super-rational God, Brahman, Atman, Tao, or its equivalent—the major premise of the ideational supersystem. (c) True value and reality are an infinite manifold, partly super-sensory and partly super-rational, partly rational, and partly sensory—the premise of the idealistic supersystem (1947: 590).

Three kinds of value systems thus characterize cultures, societies, and personalities: sensate systems, based on the premise that sensation validates belief; ideational systems, based on the premise that supernatural forces validate belief; and idealistic systems, based on the premise that belief is partly validated by sensation and partly validated by faith. The three supersystems that emerge, then, are empiricism (science), supernaturalism (religion), and rationality (logic). Thus, within each supersystem, empiricism, faith, or rationality will be seen as the key to knowledge. Sorokin examined thousands of works of art, and thus was able to identify the supersystem associated with broad historical periods in western culture: i.e., the ideational art of the early Greeks, the sensational work of the Greek classicists (e.g., *Oedipus*), the ideational works of the early Christians, changing to idealistic and then sensational by the 16th century, and so forth. Sorokin's method is therefore one of holistic interrelations (as were those of Spengler and Comte); all of the "isms" of a period are traced back to the supersystem of which they are constituent parts. The effect of all on all must be traced.

Social change can be understood in terms of immanent causes and limits. Immanent causes of change are those inherent in the system itself: "whether the system is scientific or religious, aesthetic or philosophical, whether it is represented by a family, a business firm, an occupational union, or a state, it bears within itself the seeds of incessant change. . . . Through this incessant generation of consequences attending each of its changes a system perceptibly determines that character and course of its own future career. The whole series of changes it undergoes throughout its existence is to a large extent *an unfolding of its inherent potentialities*. From an acorn can spring only an oak (696–697)." Limits are those counterforces that build up during the course of change and eventually alter the direction of that change.

> These principles sum up what we have met in the study of the fluctuations of virtually all the preceding social, cultural, and personal processes. We have observed that social organization, differentiation, and stratification grow immanently until they reach their optimum point in a given group; when the optimum point is exceeded, groups generate forces that inhibit further differentiation and stratification. On the other hand, when immobility persists too long, social systems generate forces working for differentiation. If systems do not succeed in regaining their optimum equilibrium, they tend to disintegrate. The same immanent reaction of systems and the same fluctuation between the observed limits have been observed in the alternations of freedom and re-

straint, of expansion and contraction of government regulation, of increase and decrease of
mobility, etc. (704). . . .

It follows that cultural systems do not die; they merely
change form: ". . . The basic forms of almost all sociocultural phenomena are limited in their number; hence they
inevitably recur in time, in rhythmic fashion, and in the
course of their changes do not follow a strictly linear trend"
(701). The supersystems fluctuate historically between
sensate and ideational forms, with the idealistic supersystem occupying an intermediate position. Sorokin (700, 703)
explicitly rejects both linear and cyclical theories of social
change, the former on the ground that the principles of immanent change and limits "preclude the possibility of limit-
less linear trends," [1] the latter because "in systems with a
*large number of main variants the rhythm is so complex,
consisting of so many phases, that we can hardly grasp its
nature or observe its recurrence*. . . . Thus the total change
of most systems . . . is in part a repetition of the old, and
in part ever new. The new factors preclude a recurrence
of identical cycles." Thus, "understood in the above sense,
the dominant form of the direction of sociocultural processes is neither permanently cyclical nor permanently linear, but varyingly recurrent, with incessant modifications
of the old themes" (703).

Sorokin argued that the whole could be explained only
in terms of the whole and that the sociologist must use
sociocultural supersystems as his datum, rather than groups,
nations, or even cultures. This grandiose sweep provided
Sorokin with insights that often escape more empirically
minded researchers; it also rendered his theory conceptually
difficult and operationally unmanageable. Sorokin, for example, felt that empiricism was inadequate to the understanding of supersystems, but since he was himself a
creature of a sensate culture, his own knowledge and

---

[1] This is reinforced by the fact that systems don't exist in a
vacuum; they are forever subjected to external influences. Sorokin
also cites empirical evidence to substantiate his theoretical position.

methodology could not but reflect that culture. Hence, the
derivation of his theory is grounded in a paradox.[2]

Max Weber's approach to social change was derived
from his theory of social action and, in focus and content,
differs from that of the other theorists considered in this
book. Whereas Spencer, Durkheim, and Marx, for example,
addressed themselves directly to questions of social organization, Weber was largely concerned with the types of
legitimacy characteristic of different social orders, the forms
of organization characteristic of each type, and their sources
of instability. Weber's (1964: 115) analysis of social change
departs from his classification of types of social action:

> Social action, like other forms of action, may be
> classified in the following four types according to
> its mode of orientation: (1) in terms of rational
> orientation to a system of discrete individual
> ends (*Zweckrational*), that is, through expecta-
> tions as to the behavior of objects in the external
> situation and of other human individuals, making
> use of these expectations as "conditions" or
> "means" for the successful attainment of the ac-
> tor's own rationally chosen ends; (2) in terms of
> rational orientation to an absolute value (*Wert-
> rational*); involving a conscious belief in the ab-
> solute value of some ethical, aesthetic, religious,
> or other form of behavior, entirely for its own
> sake and independently of any prospects of ex-
> ternal success; (3) in terms of affectual orienta-
> tion, especially emotional, determined by the spe-
> cific affects and states of feeling of the actor; (4)
> traditionally oriented, through the habituation of
> long practice.

These four modes of orientation in turn give rise to four
bases of legitimacy for any social order:

> Legitimacy may be ascribed to an order by
> those acting subject to it in the following ways:—

[2] This is not unique to Sorokin, of course. Marx was himself a
product of capitalist society, born into the bourgeoisie; how, then,
could he formulate a theory which itself was not distorted by virtue
of its class origins?

(a) By tradition; a belief in the legitimacy of what has always existed; (b) by virtue of affectual attitudes, especially emotional, legitimizing the validity of what is newly revealed or a model to imitate; (c) by virtue of a rational belief in its absolute value,[3] thus lending it the validity of an absolute and final commitment; (d) because it has been established in a manner which is recognized to be *legal*. This legality may be treated as legitimate in either of two ways: on the one hand, it may derive from a voluntary agreement of the interested parties on the relevant terms. On the other hand, it may be imposed on the basis of what is held to be a legitimate authority over the relevant persons and a corresponding claim to their obedience (130).

Authority,[4] then, insofar as it is legitimate, is seen by Weber (328) as resting on either rational, traditional, or charismatic grounds:

[3] *Wertrational.*

[4] "Authority" or "legitimate authority" is used when Weber talks of *legitime Herrschaft. Herrschaft*, somewhat awkwardly translated as "imperative control," is defined by Weber as "the probability that a command with a specific content will be obeyed by a given group of persons." (p. 152. See also footnote 83, p. 152, in which Parsons discusses the difficulties of translating *Herrschaft*.) The concept of authority is developed by Weber in the context of the corporate group (*Verband*), defined as "a social relationship which is either closed or limits the admission of outsiders by rules." (p. 145). The corporate group is distinguished by role differentiation with respect to authority —membership from leadership, and, within the latter category, the "chief" (*Leiter*) from the "administrative staff" (*Verwaltungsstab*). Parsons observes that "it is safe to hold that Weber considered this basic structure to be normal for groups of any size and complexity in all fields of routine human action." (p. 56). It is in this context, then, that Weber develops his analysis of the types of (imperatively controlled) social organizations characteristic of the three bases of legitimation of authority. It should be noted, of course, that Weber regarded the three types of legitimate authority as pure or ideal types, not necessarily to be found in actuality: "The fact that none of these three ideal types . . . is usually to be found in historical cases in 'pure' form, is naturally not a valid objection to attempting their conceptual formulation in the sharpest possible form . . . the idea that the whole of concrete historical reality can be exhausted in the conceptual scheme about to be developed is as far from the author's thoughts as anything could be." (p. 329). For a discussion of Weber's methodology, see Parsons' (1964: 8–29) introduction to Weber.

There are three pure types of legitimate authority. The validity of their claims to legitimacy may be based on:

1. Rational grounds—resting on a belief in the "legality" of patterns of normative rules and the right of those elevated to authority under such rules to issue commands (legal authority).

2. Traditional grounds—resting on an established belief in the sanctity of immemorial traditions and the legitimacy of the status of those exercising authority under them (traditional authority); or finally,

3. Charismatic grounds—resting on devotion to the specific and exceptional sanctity, heroism or exemplary character of an individual person, and of the normative patterns or order revealed or ordained by him (charismatic authority).

In the case of legal authority, obedience is owed to the legally established impersonal order. It extends to the persons exercising the authority of office under it only by virtue of the formal legality of their commands and only within the scope of authority of the office. In the case of traditional authority, obedience is owed to the *person* of the chief who occupies the traditionally sanctioned position of authority and who is (within its sphere) bound by tradition. But here the obligation of obedience is not based on the impersonal order, but is a matter of personal loyalty within the area of accustomed obligations. In the case of charismatic authority, it is the charismatically qualified leader as such who is obeyed by virtue of personal trust in him and his revelation, his heroism or his exemplary qualities so far as they fall within the scope of the individual's belief in his charisma.

Part III of *The Theory of Social and Economic Organization* is concerned with an examination of the three types of authority and their associated forms of social organization. Rational-legal authority is characterized by the existence of a body of generalized, universalistic, and impersonal rules which cover all cases of conduct within the group. In its pure form, rational-legal authority accrues only to the office, never to the officeholder; the individual's office is clearly separated from his private affairs.

The following may thus be said to be the fundamental categories of rational legal authority:

(1) A continuous organization of official
functions bound by rules.

(2) A specified sphere of competence. This
involves (a) a sphere of obligations to perform
functions which have been marked off as part of
a systematic division of labor. (b) The provision
of the incumbent with the necessary authority to
carry out these functions. (c) That the necessary
means of compulsion are clearly defined and their
use is subject to definite conditions. . . .

(3) The organization of offices follows the
principle of hierarchy; that is, each lower office
is under the control and supervision of a higher
one. . . .

(4) The rules which regulate the conduct of
an office may be technical rules or norms. In both
cases, if their application is to be fully rational,
specialized training is necessary. . . .

(5) In the rational type it is a matter of
principle that the members of the administrative
staff should be completely separated from ownership of the means of production or administration. . . . There exists, furthermore, in principle
complete separation of the property belonging to
the organization, which is controlled within the
sphere of office, and the personal property of the
official, which is available for his own private
uses. . . .

(6) In the rational type case, there is also a
complete absence of appropriation of his official
position by the incumbent. . . .

(7) Administrative acts, decisions, and rules
are formulated and recorded in writing, even in
cases where oral discussion is the rule or even
mandatory (330–332). . . .

In its purest form, legal authority is that which employs
a bureaucratic administrative staff. Weber's discussion of
the characteristics of bureaucracy departs directly from
the above description of rational authority.

Traditional authority is the second pure type considered
by Weber. Unlike rational authority, in which order is regarded as legitimate to the extent that it is achieved through
procedures regarded as legitimate (e.g., legislation), order,

under traditional authority, is regarded as always having
been in existence and binding. Rules are accepted because
they always have been, not because they are enacted through
legitimate procedures: "A system of imperative co-ordina-
tion will be called 'traditional' if legitimacy is claimed for
it and believed in on the basis of the sanctity of the order
and the attendant powers of control as they have been
handed down from the past, have always existed. The person or persons exercising authority are designated according to traditionally transmitted rules (341)." Legitimate
authority accrues not to the "office," but to the occupant of
a more generalized status and under specified conditions:

> The object of obedience is the personal au-
> thority of the individual which he enjoys by vir-
> tue of his traditional status. The organized group
> exercising authority is, in the simplest case, pri-
> marily based on relations of personal loyalty, cul-
> tivated through a common process of education.
> The person exercising authority is not a "su-
> perior," but a personal "chief."
> His administrative staff does not consist pri-
> marily of officials, but of personal retainers.
> Those subject to authority are not "members" of
> an association, but are either his traditional
> "comrades" or his "subjects." What determines
> the relations of the administrative staff to the
> chief is not the impersonal obligation of office,
> but personal loyalty to the chief.
> Obedience is not owed to enacted rules, but
> to the person who occupies a position of authority
> by tradition or who has been chosen for such a
> position on a traditional basis. His commands are
> legitimized in one of two ways: (a) partly in
> terms of traditions which themselves directly de-
> termine the content of the command and the ob-
> jects and extent of authority. In so far as this is
> true, to overstep the traditional limitations would
> endanger his traditional status by undermining
> acceptance of his legitimacy. (b) In part, it is a
> matter of the chief's free personal decision, in
> that tradition leaves a certain sphere open for
> this. This sphere of traditional prerogative rests
> primarily on the fact that the obligations of obe-
> dience on the basis of personal loyalty are es-

sentially unlimited. There is thus a double sphere:
on the one hand, of action which is bound to specific tradition; on the other hand, of that which
is free of any specific rules (341–342).

The third pure type of authority, charismatic, differs
from the other two in its non-routine, revolutionary character. Both traditional and rational authority are regarded
by Weber as essentially stable and routinized. Charismatic
authority arises in precise opposition to such routinized
social order and attempts to substitute a new order based
on unquestioning, unlimited loyalty to the charismatic
leader.

> Charismatic authority is thus specifically out-
> side the realm of everyday and the profane
> sphere. In this respect, it is sharply opposed both
> to rational, and particularly bureaucratic, au-
> thority, and to traditional authority, whether in
> its patriarchal, patrimonial, or any other form.
> Both rational and traditional authority are spe-
> cifically forms of everyday routine control of ac-
> tion; while the charismatic type is the direct an-
> tithesis of this. Bureaucratic authority is spe-
> cifically rational in the sense of being bound to
> intellectually analysable rules; while charismatic
> authority is specifically irrational in the sense of
> being foreign to all rules. Traditional authority
> is bound to the precedents handed down from the
> past and to this extent is also oriented to rules.
> Within the sphere of its claims, charismatic au-
> thority repudiates the past, and is in this sense a
> specifically revolutionary force. It recognizes no
> appropriation of positions of power by virtue of
> the possession of property, either on the part of
> a chief or of socially privileged groups. The only
> basis of legitimacy for it is personal charisma, so
> long as it is proved; that is, as long as it receives
> recognition and is able to satisfy the followers or
> disciples. But this lasts only so long as the belief
> in its charismatic inspiration remains (361–362).

The charismatic leader is regarded by his followers as being
endowed with "supernatural, superhuman, or at least specifically exceptional powers or qualities" (358). His legit-

imacy is based in the conception that it is the *duty* of his
followers to unstintingly obey all commands. "There is no
system of formal rules, of abstract legal principles, and
hence no process of judicial decision oriented to them. But
equally there is no legal wisdom oriented to judicial prece-
dent. Formally concrete judgments are newly created from
case to case and are originally regarded as divine judgments
and revelations. From a substantive point of view, every
charismatic authority would have to subscribe to the proposition, 'It is written . . . , but I say unto you. . . .' (361)."
The administrative staff of the charismatic authority is
chosen on the basis of the charismatic qualities of its members. "There is no such thing as 'appointment' or 'dis-
missal,' no career, no promotion. There is only a 'call' at
the instance of the leader on the basis of the charismatic
qualification of those he summons. There is no hierarchy;
the leader merely intervenes in general or in individual
cases when he considers the members of his staff inadequate
to a task with which they have been entrusted" (360). Just
as there is no concept of office, there is no concept of econ-
omizing or of routine income-producing activities; financial
support is attained through gifts or coercion.

In its pure form, charismatic authority is clearly unstable and Weber devotes considerable attention to the process by which charisma is routinized. The initial problem,
of course, deals with succession: who shall replace the
leader, and how shall his status be legitimized? Various
alternatives including hereditary succession, designation by
the leader or his staff, and revelation are delineated. Similar
questions arise with regard to the leader's staff, which
cannot exist long on a purely *ad hoc* basis. Regularization
may occur in a traditional direction (developing tradition-
alized statuses) or in a rational direction (developing
offices). Finally, some form of stable economic support of
the leader and his staff is necessary; this is achieved by
instituting a system of compulsory obligations (such as
taxes) that, in turn, limit the freedom of the subject
groups. Thus, "for charisma to be transformed into a permanent routine structure, it is necessary that its anti-eco-

nomic character be altered. It must be adapted to some form of fiscal organization to provide for the needs of the group and hence to the economic conditions necessary for raising taxes and contributions. . . . as soon as control over large masses of people exists, it gives way to the forces of everyday routine" (369–370).

Weber's theory of social change envisions an oscillation between the three kinds of authority. We have seen how charismatic authority tends to be a revolutionary force,[5] overthrowing rational or traditional bases of authority and replacing them with a new basis that is itself unstable. Charismatic authority, as suggested above, tends to become routinized over time either in a traditional or a rational direction, according to the historical conditions under which it arises. In Webers' view, neither legal, traditional, nor charismatic authority is inherently stable. In terms of social organization, traditional authority is treated as being the most stable, as rational authority tends to break down into traditional or charismatic forms. Traditional authority, however, is itself seen as eroding under the impact of a long-run trend towards rationalization in the Western hemisphere—a process that provided the subject of much of Weber's empirical work, which will be considered shortly. The sources of instability in charismatic authority, tending towards its routinization, have already been discussed. Rational authority tends to break down for several reasons,[6] reflecting the strains inherent in the rational form of social organization. Talcott Parsons (1964), in his introduction to *The Theory of Social and Economic Organization*, identifies such sources of strain:

[5] Although Weber refers to a chapter on the theory of revolutions, Parsons notes that this chapter was apparently never written and that a systematic account of revolutions is not available in Weber's published works.

[6] Rational authority can, of course, give way to either traditional or charismatic authority. Unfortunately, Weber was not so concerned about the sources of charismatic movements as he was their subsequent development and routinization, so it is difficult to specify the conditions under which rational authority is replaced by the one or the other. See Parsons' (1964: 68–77) introduction to *The Theory of Social and Economic Organization*.

One source of such strain [for which there is much material in Weber's discussion and observations] is the segregation of roles, and of the corresponding authority to use influence over others and over non-human resources, which is inherent in the functionally limited sphere of office. There are always tendencies to stretch the sanctioned limits of official authority to take in ranges of otherwise "personal" interests. . . . A particular case of this is the tendency of persons in authority to claim obedience, and for this claim to be recognized, on a personal basis, as John Jones, rather than on the basis of office as such. It is then not the impersonal order which is being obeyed, but the personal prestige of the incumbent. The segregation required by rational-legal authority is subtle and difficult to maintain. . . . The tendency to break down the segregation between the official and the personal spheres will [thus probably result] in the increase of institutionalization of individual functions and status in the "total" status form, in other words, of features Weber treats as typical of traditional authority.

A second fundamental consideration is that discipline and authority, probably always in any large-scale permanent system, generate various forms of resistance and resentment. . . . The very fact that the [rational] sphere of authority is functionally limited deprives it of the support of certain motives which contribute to the solidarity of other systems, notably motives of personally loyal attachment to particular individuals and *Gemeinschaft* groups. Above all, for a variety of reasons, it tends to generate widespread feelings of insecurity. . . .

The probability is then that a breakdown of rational-legal authority through successful defiance of it on the part of its "objects" will result in its gradual replacement by other forms, notably the traditional. . . .

"Reason" is, as Weber several times remarks, an inherently dynamic force subject to continual change, and hence has a strong tendency not to permit the development of settled routines and symbolic associations which would minimize psychological strain.

Weber's theory of social change must be considered in light of his empirical works on long-run cultural evolution in the west, in which he traced the process of increasing rationalization in a variety of institutional spheres. Weber (1958: 13) felt that western civilization was unique in that scientific rationality had pervaded other areas of life to an extent unprecedented elsewhere, a theme which he sets forth in his introduction to *The Protestant Ethic and the Spirit of Capitalism*:

A product of modern European civilization, studying any problem of universal history, is bound to ask himself to what combination of circumstances the fact should be attributed that in Western civilization, and in Western civilization only, cultural phenomena have appeared which (as we like to think) lie in a line of development having *universal* significance and value.

Only in the west does science exist at a stage of development which we recognize today as valid.

Although some phases of knowledge and scientific observation have been highly developed elsewhere (particularly in India, China, Babylonia, and Egypt), scientific rationality has always been underdeveloped in some respects. This is true of astronomy, the natural sciences, and medicine. It is true of historical scholarship, political thought, and law. It is even true of music and architecture:

. . . rational harmonious music, both counterpoint and harmony, formation of the tone material on the basis of three triads with the harmonic third; our chromatics and enharmonics, not interpreted in terms of space, but, since the Renaissance, of harmony; our orchestra, with its string quartet as a nucleus, and the organization of ensembles of wind instruments; our bass accompaniment; our system of notation, which has made possible the composition and production of modern musical works, and thus their very survival; our sonatas, symphonies, operas; and finally, as means to all these, our fundamental instruments, the organ, piano, violin, etc.; all these

things are known only in the Occident, although
programme music, tone poetry, alteration of tones
and chromatics, have existed in various musical
traditions as means of expression.

In architecture, pointed arches have been
used elsewhere as a means of decoration, in an-
tiquity and in Asia; presumably the combination
of pointed arch and cross-arched vault was not
unknown in the Orient. But the rational use of
the Gothic vault as a means of distributing pres-
sure and of roofing spaces of all forms, and above
all as the constructive principle of great monu-
mental buildings and the foundation of a *style*
extending to sculpture and painting, such as that
created by our Middle Ages, does not occur elsewhere (14–15).

Weber (17) was, of course, most concerned with the
increasing rationalization of the economic sphere and its
manifestation in Western capitalistic enterprise:

And the same is true of the most fateful force in
our modern life, capitalism. . . . The impulse to
acquisition, pursuit of gain, of money, of the
greatest possible amount of money, has in itself
nothing to do with capitalism. . . . Unlimited
greed for gain is not in the least identical with
capitalism, and is still less its spirit. Capitalism
may even be identical with the restraint, or at
least a rational tempering, of this irrational impulse. But capitalism is identical with the pursuit
of profit, by means of continuous, rational, capitalistic enterprise.

Rudimentary forms of capitalism[7] can be found outside the
Western civilization, but, only in the west did it develop in
the direction of rational capitalistic organization, built
around free markets for both products and factors of production (especially labor), with the concomitant separation of
business from the household, and the use of rational book-
keeping—the hallmarks of modern capitalism which dis-

---

[7] Weber (1964: 17) defines a capitalistic economic action as "one
which rests on the expectation of profit by the utilization of opportunities for exchange, that is on (formally) peaceful chances of
profit."

tinguish it from earlier pre-capitalistic forms. Weber identifies the rational ethic associated with the early development
of capitalism in the west as Calvinism, whose this-worldly
asceticism facilitated the development of the western capitalist entrepreneur.

Thus, Weber sees a long run evolution in the direction
of increasing rationalization in all areas of life, a process
which includes increasing rationalization of social organization. But rational-legal authority is seen as less stable than
traditional authority, susceptible to both traditionalization
in specific areas and to the appeal of charismatic movements. The prognosis, then, would appear to be substantial
instability and not infrequent shifts between the three types
of authority. Writing of capitalism, Weber (182) has said:

> No one knows who will live in this cage in
> the future, or whether at the end of this tremen-
> dous development entirely new prophets will
> arise, or there will be a great rebirth of old ideas
> and ideals, or, if neither, mechanized petrification,
> embellished with a sort of convulsive self-impor-
> tance. For of the last stage of this cultural de-
> velopment, it might well be truly said: "Special-
> ists without spirit, sensualists without heart; this
> nullity imagines that it has attained a level of
> civilization never before achieved."

REFERENCES

Etzioni, Amitai, and Eva Etzioni, eds.
   1964   Social Change. New York: Basic Books.
Parsons, Talcott.
   1964   "Introduction." In Max Weber, The Theory of So-
           cial and Economic Organization. New York: Free
           Press.
Sorokin, Pitirim A.
   1931   Social and Cultural Dynamics. 2 vols. Bedminster.
   1947   Society, Culture, and Personality. New York:
           Harper & Row.
Spengler, Oswald.
   1964   "The Life cycle of cultures." In Amitai and Eva

Etzioni, eds. Social Change. New York: Basic Books.

Weber, Max.
1958   The Protestant Ethic and the Spirit of Capitalism. New York: Scribner.
1964   The Theory of Social and Economic Organization. New York: Free Press.

5

Classification and Study of Theories of Social Change

The classification of theories presented in the preceding chapters has grown out of similar efforts on the part of other students of social change. In this final chapter, several such efforts are briefly reviewed and evaluated in light of the present classification. We shall conclude with an overview and appraisal of the principal theoretical approaches to the study of social change.

THE STUDY OF SOCIAL CHANGE

The State of the Field as Seen by Several Major Theorists

Wilbert E. Moore, in his article on social change in the *International Encyclopedia of the Social Sciences* (1968: 367–368) distinguishes four classes of theories, which he presents as "changing theoretical interests," presumably in chronological order of dominance over the field. The first major grouping consists of evolutionary theories and is characterized by much of the sociological theorizing typical of the late 19th century, following the discoveries of Charles Darwin. Major proponents of social evolutionism include Spencer and Morgan, although Moore notes the importance of evolutionary theory in the works of Sumner and Durkheim as well. Evolutionary theories, for Moore, are characterized by notions of the increasing complexity and structural differentiation of society, along with some concept of directionality in change ("progress"). The former concept is crucial, however, and it appears that Moore (367, italics added) is willing to subsume "directionality" under increasing complexity: "the directionality of change, and *in particular* the increasing complexity and structural differentiation of society, came to be a major tenet of evolutionary theories." If evolutionists are thus defined in terms of the assumption that societies move in the direction of increasing complexity, there are few social theorists of the 19th or 20th century who would escape such a classification. Moore recognizes this, for he notes that his second historical class of theories—Marxism—was in reality a variant of evolutionism, while his third class—functionalism—was initially associated with Durkheim's works, which were dominated by the then current evolutionary theories. Marxism is held to be a variant of evolutionism on several accounts. It adheres to the notion of sequential stages of social organization and conceives of social change as largely due to impersonal and inevitable forces playing on social organizations. Marx apparently differs with the evolutionists, however, in that "his theory was a dynamic one (367)," however much it underplayed the role of ideas and values. Functionalism, the third stage, attempts to explain phenomena that are quasi-simultaneous. Its fundamental tenet is that the different parts of the social structure are interdependant and hence, to an extent, self-equilibrating. Functionalism is similar to evolutionism in the assumption that all modern societies have essentially the same kind of social structure, e.g., "modernization" implies movement in the same direction for all societies. Unlike evolutionary theories, however, functionalist theories tend to be "before and after" theories, rather than process theories. Functionalism, in viewing society as a "functional equilibrium system," is able to make predictions concerning the correlations among selected variables. In its most sophisticated form, it views society as a tension-management system, making order itself problematic: function is combined with the notion of dysfunction, equilibrium with disequilibrium, and order with tension-managment. The final type of theory, clearly not on a par with the others in Moore's view, is confiict theory (see Dahrendorf, 1959) ; although a "viable alternative" to functionalism, it does not seem to be "a comprehensive construction," as much as a change of emphasis (from social integration to discordance) and, as such, adds little to the tension-management variant of functional theories.

Moore, in his brief discussion, sets up classes of theories but fails to indicate adequately how they differ from one another. The few observations he offers seem designed to indicate the similarity between Marxism, functionalism, and evolutionism. His insight that all the theories emphasize increasing structural complexity (and structural interdependence) is one which has been incorporated into our analysis.

Neil J. Smelser (1967: ch. 12; see also 1968: ch. 8) reviews and criticizes several theories of social change under the general topic "approaches to social change." He claims his categorization of approaches is neither exhaustive nor inclusive of all major theorists. His major purpose is to give an "illustrative sample" of approaches to change and show how they can be criticized. The first category is classical evolutionary theory, whose proponents include Comte, Maine, and Morgan. For Smelser (1967: 705), the defining characteristic of evolutionary theories is that they stress "progressive evolution from lower to higher forms," that civilizations progress from a backward to an advanced state. Thus, there is Comte's movement from the theological through the metaphysical to the positivist state; Maine's progress from the patriarchal, status-oriented social order to the libertarian, contractual order; and Morgan's "human progress from savagery through barbarism to civilization" (from the title of his book). Classical evolutionism raised innumerable objections, mostly centering about its basis in untestable, value-laden assertions that, in many cases, failed to square with empirical (mainly anthropological) research. It was in reaction to evolutionism that several of the other approaches emerged at the turn of the 20th century. All other theories reviewed by Smelser are classified as alternatives to evolutionism. The alternatives are several. Ogburn (1922: 57), for example, offered cultural lag theory, claiming that classical evolutionary theory "has not only not been proven but has been disproven." According to Ogburn, material culture (most notably, inventions) proceeds at a faster rate of change than adaptive culture (customs, beliefs, philosophies, laws, governments), resulting in a continuous social maladjustment.

Classical diffusion theory, associated with anthropologists such as Kroeber, is another alternative to evolutionism discussed by Smelser. Diffusionists rejected the often implicit assumption of evolutionists that societies develop according to a purely internal adaptation to environment, what Smelser (1967: 705) terms a "single-line, immanent view of cultural change." In its place, they emphasized the empirical interrelations among societies and how societies as a consequence "borrow" from one another. Diffusionists focused almost entirely on the movement of *things* among societies and were little concerned with the social-system contexts of such movement. They were ethnographers, not sociologists, and as a consequence their work has received little acceptance among sociological students of change.

Classical functionalism is another alternative. Functionalism proceeds by analogy to the living organism in its interrelatedness among the parts: each unit is necessary (functional) for the successful operation of the whole. Functionalism, therefore, accounts for a given pattern of activities by reference to the social system of which it is a part. Smelser's discussion of functionalism is similar to Moore's. The critical points raised are that functionalism, insofar as it is a form of equilibrium theory, focuses excessively on stability and harmony, and that this difficulty is not endemic to the theory itself, and indeed has been remedied with such notions as "dysfunction" and "strain."

The fourth alternative discussed by Smelser is multi-linear evolution, a theory identified with Steward. Multi-linear evolution, simply enough, asserts a multiplicity of patterns of evolution, rather than a simple unilinear model to which all societies at all times must conform. The key task, then, is to identify these patterns and assign individual societies to each. Steward's approach is thus a more empirically accurate approach than classical evolution. It fits better with the facts but, like diffusion theory, tends to be descriptive rather than theoretical.

"Rise and fall" theories are the final approach considered by Smelser. These theories focus on the development, maturity, and decline of great civilizations, and they emphasize cyclical patterns, rather than cumulative ones. Sorokin, Spengler, and Toynbee are names associated with this type of theory. The notion that cultures or civilizations may decline as well as evolve is an important one, so this class of theory has been incorporated into our classificatory schema.

Amitai and Eva Etzioni's (1964) treatment of theories of social change is not as systematic as that of Moore and Smelser; the organization of their book is undoubtedly designed to facilitate reference rather than to provide a comprehensive classification of theories. The two broad categories of patterns of change include classical theories—the evolutionary theories of Spencer and Comte, the life cycle theories of Spengler and Toynbee, and the works of Marx, Weber, and Toennies—and modern theories, exemplified by functionalism, conflict theories, neoevolutionism, diffusionism, cybernetic theories, folk-urban theories, and need-achievement theories. There is also a section on modernization which might be considered another category of theories. The Etzionis thus offer some additional categories to be subsumed under more general headings—categories such as folk-urban (a type of modernization theory), cybernetics (another name for system theory), and the focus on modernization as a category.[1]

[1] No attempt is made to integrate the categories thus identified into a single, overarching, analytical framework.

An Alternative Schema

Of the three typologies reviewed above, Moore's classification represents the principal effort to do more than offer a checklist of major theories.[2] The four categories offered by Moore, evolutionary theories, Marxist theories, functional theories, and conflict theories, appear to be reasonable in a sort of intuitive way; the category labels are familiar ones in the sociological literature and the ordering of categories corresponds roughly to the historical sequence of predominant schools in sociology (the last category, recently emerged, has not achieved predominance and is found wanting in Moore's view). A closer inspection of this categorization raises some questions, however, regarding the underlying principle of categorization. If one accepts Moore's characterization of evolutionary theories in terms of increasing complexity and structural differentiation of societies, all of the theories he considers are in some sense variants of this underlying type. Moore, in acknowledging this problem, appears to argue that the differences among the four categories are sufficiently great to warrant the classification, despite the underlying similarity. While such a procedure is acceptable, it is not clear in this case exactly what such significant differences are. Marxism, for example, is held to differ from evolutionism by virtue of its emphasis on the "dynamic" aspects of social change; yet conflict theory, characterized as focusing on discordance rather than on integration, clearly is "dynamic" in the same way as is Marxism (Dahrendorf considers himself to be a sociological descendent of Marx). Functionalism, held by Moore to constitute the dominant paradigm today, differs from evolutionism in its emphasis on homeostasis; yet Durkheim, the father of functionalism, was clearly an early evolutionist. What appears to differentiate these categories

[2] A recent essay by Smelser (1967) offers a four-fold classification based on time horizon and direction of change. Such dimensioning, which focuses on the *change* aspect of social change, may prove to be especially useful in the synthesis of several approaches to change into a single unified one; this indeed is a primary purpose of Smelser's essay. The classifications reviewed above, like that offered in the text, focus also on the *social* aspect of social change—i.e., the underlying assumptions about society which appear to determine the categories identified in the classification.

for Moore is their respective *emphases;* while they are all compatible with the assumption that societies develop in the direction of greater structural complexity (the principal contribution of the 19th century evolutionists), they depart from this assumption in significant ways. Some theories depart in emphasizing the discordance and discontinuity of change—the "dynamic" aspects of change. Such theories are classified as Marxist theories or conflict theories. Others emphasize the harmonious aspects of change by regarding society as a self-equilibrating, homeostatic system; much of the emphasis of contemporary functionalism (particularly what has come to be called systems theory) is in this direction. Thus, while one may not agree with Moore's precise categorizations, the principle which appears to underlie those categorizations appears to be useful. That principle, whether or not stability is assumed to underlie social organization and social change, gives rise to three groupings that differ in their underlying assumptions regarding such stability: equilibrium theories, evolutionary theories, and conflict theories. The former *emphasizes* stability at the expense of change; the latter *emphasizes* change at the expense of stability; the middle grouping *emphasizes* neither, assuming change to be harmonious and continuous. Since these are questions of relative emphasis, a single theoretical approach may contain specific variants that fall into different groups according to the prevalent emphasis. Thus, systems theory, as developed by Parsons, focuses on boundary relations between social subsystems that tend generally towards equilibrium at the societal level, while modernization theory, as exemplified by Levy, focuses on the evolutionary changes that result from the impact of industrialization on functionally interdependent social systems. Both approaches agree that the underlying process of change is one of differentiation, specialization, and reintegration; both are thus evolutionary theories in that fundamental sense, although systems theory then proceeds to focus on equilibrium in boundary exchanges while modernization theory is primarily concerned with the ramifications of the evolutionary process itself.

Smelser's classification is apparently intended to serve

as a checklist for types of theory that emerged in response to 19th century "classical" evolutionary theory (Comte, Maine, and Morgan). Such theories are considered largely in terms of how they built on and/or surpassed evolutionism. The Etzionis follow a similar procedure in organizing their reader on social change, although their principal distinction appears to be chronological—19th century ("classical") versus 20th century ("modern").[3] Since both of these classifications are intended to provide wide coverage of the literature rather than remain rigorously faithful to some explicit underlying organizational principle, they do succeed in covering types of theories not explicitly mentioned by Moore. Smelser, for example, discusses cultural lag theory, diffusion theory, multilinear evolution, and rise and fall theories, while the Etzioni reader covers (in addition to these) folk-urban theories and need-achievement theories. These classifications are primarily useful in reminding the reader of the breadth of the field and calling attention to the difficulties inherent in organizing a classificatory schema based on a single underlying principle (such as assumptions regarding stability) that will somehow manage to cover all the important works on social change.

In particular, the three categories derived from Moore appear to be insufficient to include at least one major category of theories—those which do *not* adhere to the underlying assumption that change is uniform in direction. Such theories, termed life cycle theories by Etzioni and rise and fall theories by Smelser, emphasize decay as well as progress and must be incorporated into any schema which hopes to be complete. In addition, certain other theorists are handled with difficulty by a classification scheme organized according to whether principal emphasis is on equilibrium, evolutionary development, or conflict. Some writers might reasonably be excluded on the grounds that their focus was on individual or group processes alleged to underlie such change rather than on the social system aspect of social change. Thus, McClelland's (1961) theories of achievement

[3] The reader is actually divided into several sections in addition to the two noted above, but the organizing principle is not entirely clear to this writer. The other sections include modernization, spheres of change, levels of change, and processes of change.

motivation and Hagen's (1962) extension (and empirical application) of these theories to several developing societies are primarily concerned with the development of high achievement-motivated individuals who subsequently come to dominate the key developmental sectors of their nation's economies. While the social conditions motivating the development of such individuals are of some concern, the issue of the societal-level changes that accompany or promote economic change is not of central interest to these theorists. Their emphasis, in fact, tends to be on the childhood socialization and social marginality of the entrepreneur-type individual and group.

Other writers, however, are not so easily excluded from the schema, even though they do not appear to fit neatly within it; the most important such writer is Max Weber. Weber has been classified as a "rise and fall" theorist with some reluctance, for his writings on social change in many respects bridge the different categories. Nevertheless, as Etzioni (1964: 5) notes, "Weber's approach to change is two-pronged; he combines a cyclical theory of social development with a linear theory of cultural development." The modern state, for Weber, alternates between periods in which legitimacy is grounded in tradition and those in which legitimacy is grounded in rational-legal authority. The charismatic leader provides the dynamic; as the prevailing form of legitimacy is eroded, the charismatic leader emerges, offering a new foundation for legitimacy—which, in turn, eventually becomes routinized in a traditional or rational-legal direction. At the cultural level, however, as Etzioni (1964: 5) observes, Weber sees a linear development much as the evolutionary theorists saw at the social level. Western culture is seen as developing in the direction of ever increasing rationality, consistency, and coherence. This theme provides the basis for much of Weber's empirical work, in which he traced the progress of rationalism in such areas as science, art, architecture, literature, and economic organization. Thus, with Weber, it is possible to analytically separate the social system level from the cultural system level.[4] In his treatment of social systems he is classi-

[4] See Introduction, above.

fied with those theorists who perceive no uniform linear development, although in his treatment of cultural systems he might well be classified as an evolutionist.

Our classification, then, represents an outgrowth of those developed by the writers reviewed above. It is organized along two principal dimensions of social change, one related to the "social," the other to "change." The "social" dimension is concerned with the degree to which social organization is perceived as possessing inherent stability. The "change" dimension is concerned with whether or not all societies at all times are perceived as moving in a uniform "direction"—however generally direction may be defined. The resulting classification may be depicted as follows:

CHANGE: directionality of change	SOCIAL: underlying assumptions concerning inherent stability of societal organization		
	inherently stable, little attention given to change	inherently stable, but seen as changing smoothly	inherently unstable, little attention given to stability
YES: theoretical focus is on uniformities in direction of change	equilibrium theory	evolutionary theory	conflict theory
NO: theoretical focus is on lack of uniformities in direction of change	rise-and-fall theories (Spengler, Sorokin)		(Weber)

Several features of this classification should be noted. The difference between evolutionary theories and equilibrium theories, as mentioned previously, is largely one of emphasis; the latter focus on social mechanisms that tend to restore equilibrium in the face of (generally exogenous) disturbances, while the former focus on the process of change itself. These are two sides of the same coin, and the difference is more analytic than real. Parsons, for example, has written essays with an evolutionary focus (1966; 1960: ch. 3), as well as essays with an equilibrium focus (Parsons and Smelser, 1965; Parsons, 1960: ch. 4). Conflict theories, on the other hand, are quite distinct from those of the other two categories. For conflict theorists, the resolution of opposing interests occurs through their mutual annihilation and the emergence of new forms of social organization —a new synthesis that is quite different from the "working out" of conflict assumed by equilibrium and evolutionary theorists. For the evolutionist, stability is the keynote and change is regarded as essentially smooth, continuous, and incremental; for the equilibrium theorist, instability is assumed and change tends to be abrupt, discontinuous, and total. Rise and fall theories seem to cut across the "inherently stable but changing smoothly" and the "inherently unstable" categories. They share with conflict theories the assumption that societies contain within themselves the seeds of their own future decay (Spengler's analogy with the human organism, Sorokin's "limits"), but unlike conflict theories, they do not view such decay as necessarily cataclysmic or abrupt. Perhaps Weber can be more properly classified in the "inherently unstable" category than either Spengler or Sorokin, for Weber (1964: 361–362) sees charisma as an irrational revolutionary force, the antithesis of the routine control of action characteristic of both traditional and rational authority.

THEORIES OF SOCIAL CHANGE

"Theory" has been described by Homans (1950: 3, see fn. 5) as the form in which the results of observation may be expressed. It is thus a generalized conceptualization, a body of logically interdependent generalized concepts with empirical reference (Parsons, 1954: 212). Parsons has identified two functions of theory, description and analysis. Analysis involves causal explanation and the generation of general laws (212). The theories we have considered in the preceding chapters are general theories concerned with dynamic analysis. They begin with observation of data and proceed to the deduction of general propositions regarding the relationships among variables. These propositions are often in the form of causal explanations as they specify a set of necessary and/or sufficient conditions for the occurrence of a specified event (e.g., Durkheim's proposition that increasing moral density beyond a certain point produces social differentiation and hence a division of labor). The propositions thus derived form an interrelated system in that the implications of any set of propositions are explicitly stated in other propositions (212) ; ideally, they enable one to handle all theoretically relevant variables simultaneously. In assessing the major types of theories, it is advisable to consider two sorts of questions. The first concerns the nature of the theories themselves. Two queries are considered to be relevant: (1) How is society conceived as "holding together?" (2) What are the implications of this conceptualization for changes in society? The second concerns the adequacy of the theories. Again, two principal queries are formulated: (1) How well does the theory fit the facts? (2) How testable is the theory—i.e., is it possible to disprove key propositions by reference to the data? All of these questions have been touched upon at various points in preceding chapters; we shall now bring together key points in summary form.

Sociology began with evolutionary theory,[5] and much of contemporary sociology bears the imprint of the 19th century evolutionary theorists. Evolutionary theory in the 19th century drew heavily upon the biological sciences; although few theorists went so far as Comte in drawing

[5] To Comte we owe the word "sociology;" to Durkheim we can trace the sociological origins of functionalism and the method of causal resolution.

analogies between the "social organism" and its biological counterpart, the biological sciences clearly provided many models for the would-be science of society. Thus, society is seen as a highly complex organism comprised of many interrelated parts, all of which function in important ways for the maintenance of the whole. The function of each part can be assessed in terms of its overall contribution to the survival of society: evolutionary theory appears to have a built-in tendency towards viewing society as a going concern, changing only insofar as the exigencies of survival demand. Stability is the keynote, and when the evolutionary theorists sought a model to explain change, they adopted one (again, from biology) that seemed to promise relative stability and continuity in change. The Darwinian theory of evolution conceived of change as resulting from adaptability: to the extent that a species was suited to its environment, the probability of its survival was increased. Chance mutation, the exact biological mechanism of adaptation, introduced randomness into the process and insured that changes would occur over extremely long time spans. Unfortunately, no such mechanism was available, by analogy or otherwise, to the nascent science of sociology. Thus, it is understandable that the tautology implicit in the Darwinian formulation of "survival of the fittest" became axiomatic in the sociological analogue. If Darwin was aware that his theory of natural selection implied that countless adaptations did *not* survive ("dead-end mutations," he might have called them had genetic mutation been discovered in the 19th century), the early sociological evolutionists apparently were unaware of this possibility. Thus, earlier social forms were seen as evolving in the direction of 19th century industrial society; knowing the end product, it was "predicted" that earlier societies all tended in the same direction. To summarize the argument, society is an organism, with different structures (to use the term that sociologists have substituted for "organs") specializing in different aspects of survival. Since societies function relatively smoothly, some structures develop which specialize in holding things together (i.e., in "integration"). As environmental exigencies come to threaten survival, either because of conflict with other societies or because resources are inadequate to population, generally, because population is increasing, existing structures become increasingly inadequate to their assigned tasks. Here, the dynamic enters: like the embryonic human cell, social structures divide into new structures, with each new structure more specialized (and hence more adapted) than its parent. In fact, several functions performed inadequately in the parent structure are now performed separately in the new structures. As this process continues over time, "simple" or "primitive" societies become exceedingly complex "modern" ones, with many structures specialized in numerous distinguishable functions. These complex societies are so *differentiated* (in this instance, sociologists have borrowed the exact terminology from the biologists) that integration has become extremely problematic, and "what structures develop to hold society together" becomes a key question. Integration was one of Durkheim's major preoccupations, and is a major focus of sociology today.

Why does differentiation occur? "Because it must if societies are to survive" is not an entirely satisfactory answer, particularly if all societies are seen as moving in the direction of survival, and, as we have mentioned above, early evolutionary theory made little provision for the possibility that the vast majority of societies in history failed to survive because they did not experience necessary differentiations or were differentiated in a manner that resulted in *lowered* adaptability. The evolutionary explanation is better as a *post hoc* description of social change than as an analysis of the process of change itself. Even as a *post hoc* description, early evolutionary theory has been found wanting in crucial respects for it did not adequately fit the mass of anthropological data that first became available in the early twentieth century. The stages of evolution specified by writers such as Comte and Morgan simply failed to square with the facts. More seriously, however, the central postulate that characterizes all evolutionary theory, that societies develop in the direction of increasing adaptability through a process of structural-functional differentiation, and become increasingly complex over time, has been called into question by empirical research. As Moore (1963: 114) notes, "the easy assumption that societies evolved from 'simple' to 'complex' forms, and that a scale based, say, on the predominant productive technology would order all significant aspects of social organization, turned out to be unwarranted." Although "modernization" theories have remained fairly true to the central postulate of increasing complexity in societal evolution,[6] other 20th century variants of evolutionary theory have sought to relax this assumption somewhat—either through the extreme relativism of multilinear evolution or by distinguishing specific from general evolution. One can scarcely disagree with Sahlins and Service (see also White, 1949) that throughout the history of mankind, there has been a long-term trend towards greater efficiency of power utilization or even with Moore's (1963: 116) implication "that there has been a long-term increase in man's ability to adapt to and control his environment, including, possibly, his 'own' or the social environment. . . ."[7] Such formulations are extremely general, however, and must be specified to less general levels before they can be adequately tested. Key propositions in the earlier evolutionary formulations have indeed been called into question on the basis of empirical research; it remains to be seen how neoevolutionary theory will fare under such testing.

Equilibrium theory is in many respects the 20th century legacy of early evolutionary theory. It differs from its predecessor primarily in emphasis. Whereas evolutionary theory combined an organismic analogy with the sociological equivalent of Darwin's theory of the evolution of species, equilibrium theorists have limited themselves primarily to the study of the social organism in its environment.[8] As has been mentioned previously in this chapter, the two are quite compatible, and some sociologists have been classified both as evolutionary and equilibrium theorists, according

[6] They also see change as uniformly in the direction of industrialization.

[7] The second clause is clearly more doubtful than the first.

[8] Perhaps reflecting current developments in the physical sciences and in cybernetics, "the system" is now seen as a more appropriate analogue than "the organism."

to the emphasis of a particular work. Like evolutionary theorists, equilibrium theorists see societies as basically stable, smooth running organisms, highly differentiated and therefore highly complex. They go beyond the evolutionary theorists, however, in viewing societies as homeostatic, possessing "mechanisms" designed to restore equilibrium once the latter is upset. Thus, they make explicit the conservative bias that is implicit in evolutionary theory. Social systems change, but only with great difficulty; forces productive of change will tend to be met by compensating forces that offset change. In general, forces for change originate outside the system; change is exogenous, not an inevitable aspect of social organization. Values and beliefs, and the institutions in which they are embodied, are extremely durable and tend to prevent changes originating at the "bottom"[9] from affecting more general structures or the nature of the society itself. Boundary exchanges, between system (or subsystem) and environment, tend to be equilibrating, not destabilizing. In human ecology theory, each "habitat" possesses some optimal balance or stable state, its climax, and once that state is reached, further change must originate outside of that habitat.[10] Only Ogburn has made change an endemic aspect of equilibrium theory: in distinguishing material from nonmaterial culture, he was able to impute an inherent conservativism to the latter, while rendering the former a dynamic in the theory of social change. Thus, while most equilibrium theorists conceive of society in such a way as to make change unlikely, Ogburn (1968: 580) relaxes the assumption of equilibrium in a manner that makes change inevitable.

Equilibrium theories currently constitute the dominant paradigm in American sociology. Talcott Parsons has noted a convergence in sociological thought towards action theory

[9] I.e., Parsons' "conditions"—the structures which enable the society to deal directly with its (material) environment.

[10] "Habitat" is, of course, difficult to define. Even narrowly defined habitats are, in today's world, clearly interrelated; it has been argued that "virtually all members of the [human] species are [today] part of a *single* system" (Moore, 1963: 116). The more generally habitat is defined, the less testable are the propositions of human ecology theory.

and ultimately systems theory. Parsons has been criticized for formulating his propositions at a level of generality that renders them untestable. Whether or not equilibrium theories of societal change can generate truly testable propositions remains to be seen; perhaps a generation of sociologists working within the Parsonsian framework will succeed in specifying Parson's highly general propositions to a more operational level. One of the reasons for the decline of human ecology theory is to be found in the lack of testability of its central propositions. If it was analytically difficult to separate the biotic level from the cultural and other levels of human organization, it proved to be empirically impossible. Perhaps systems theory will suffer a similar fate.

Conflict theorists[11] conceive of social organization as arising in response to a scarcity of desired resources. For Marx, these resources were economic in nature—the means of subsistence, or property generally. The technologies that determine the manner in which resources are exploited also determine the social organization most appropriate to that exploitation. Industrial society is seen as organized around two principal classes—a class of capitalists, who possess the resources and the means to exploit them, and a class of workers, whose labor enables the capitalist to exploit the resources. Dahrendorf concurs in this approach but conceives of the scarce resource as power, rather than property, and applies the analysis to any imperatively coordinated association, rather than only to societies in general. Equilibrium and evolutionary theories are based on metatheoretical assumptions such as "societies are relatively persistent and stable, possessing widespread value consensus among members," but conflict theory possesses its own

---

[11] Leon Mayhew (1968: vol. 14, 580) notes that "The premise of conflict theory is that men are organisms, and as such they must compete for access to the resources of life. The struggle for existence does not occur between isolated individuals but between groups. . . . As the conflict between groups becomes stabilized or organized or regulated, we may speak of the emergence of a structured society. Society is viewed as an organizational device for relating populations of organisms to an environment, and in this sense conflict theory may be said to adopt an ecological perspective."

metatheoretical assumptions representing the reverse view in that conflict and change are seen as ubiquitous, all social organization as inherently unstable, and any unity as due largely to coercion and constraint (Dahrendorf, 1959: 161–162, 237). Conflict theory looks everywhere for sources of instability. Change, therefore, is the working out of conflict. The situation is what would be called in game theory a zero-sum situation: to the extent that one group possesses the desired resource (property, power), the other group is excluded from possession and therefore seeks to change the situation to a more favorable one.

Marx's propositions concerning the historical development of class conflict derive from his observation of historical data and seem to fit the data well. We have reviewed a number of theories which, although they begin with different assumptions, are derived from historical data which they each seem to describe reasonably well. This is possible partially because the theories are sufficiently general to preclude the testing of most propositions and partially because most social data, however precisely specified, seems subject to some interpretation, especially when the sources are historical (rather than, say, experimental). Unlike many other sociologists, however, Marx's system of propositions includes a number regarding future changes in industrial society; to the extent that these propositions entail predictions sufficiently precise to be tested, Marx, more than most other theorists of social change, leaves himself open to criticism. As noted in Chapter 3, many of Marx's predictions regarding the development of capitalism have proved to be incorrect, and he has indeed been widely criticized on this account (for an extended critique, see Dahrendorf, 1959: 36–71). Yet the central propositions in Marxist theory,[12] along with its underlying assumptions regarding the ubiquity of conflict, remain untested, and, indeed, perhaps untestable.

Rise and fall theorists are characterized by a grandiose vision. Their focus is on cultural systems as well as social systems, with "culture" broadly defined to include whole

[12] For example, that distributive change precedes normative change. See A. S. Feldman and C. Hurn (1966: 378–395).

classes of societies (western society for Spengler and Weber, sociocultural supersystems for Sorokin). They are functionalists to the extent that they conceptualize society as a set of functionally interdependent units or structures; the organismic analogy, present in some form in all of the theories we have reviewed, is also in evidence here. Although Spengler makes a direct analogy between cultures and organisms, he is less concerned with the process of specialization, differentiation, and integration than with describing parallels between the life cycle of the human organism and that of societies.[13] Sorokin and Weber, on the other hand, address themselves directly to these processes, and their terminology is more recognizably functionalist. Spengler's organicism was avowedly anti-scientific; pure analogy was seen as the proper form for the study of culture and history as living entities. Sorokin's (1947: 5) organicism was, instead, holistic: social facts are understandable only in terms of "man's sociocultural universe as a whole." Social change, for these theorists, is conceptualized in terms of the inherent limitations on the unfolding of any process: in this, rise and fall theorists resemble Marx, who felt that each historical form of social organization contained within itself the seeds of its own future demise. Spengler sees the development of living cultures into dead civilizations as analogous to the fate of individual man, the youthful spurts of energy culminating in the austere, mature adult, fated thereafter to grow old and decrepit, his potentialities long since realized, his energies sapped. Sorokin addresses himself directly to the nature of "limits," by which social groups generate counterforces to inhibit the further unfolding of processes which have reached their optimum levels. If the human ecologists saw the ecological climax as an equilibrium, departure from which required the impact of exogenous forces, Sorokin felt that no equilibrium was stable: endogenous forces resulting from the logic of the process itself would upset any equilibrium and set the process off in a new direction. Despite the fact that

[13] "Society" and "culture" are used interchangeably to refer to what Sorokin would term "sociocultural systems," a term which embraces both.

rational-legal authority was itself the product of a long-run, cumulative cultural trend in the west, Weber saw limitations on its stability that prophesy its disintegration into traditional or charismatic forms. These latter bases of legitimacy themselves are subject to limitations, the former because it is antithetical to the cultural development of rationalism, the latter because charisma must be routinized to be stable. Weber thus anticipated Ogburn in recognizing that evolutionary (or, more directly, linear) developments in one area of culture could have a permanently destabilizing effect on other areas.[14]

Of the three theorists considered in Chapter IV, Sorokin and Weber set forth propositions in a form that permits testing, although such testable propositions are the less general ones and hence less central to the authors' theoretical schemas. Sorokin's (1959) empirical work on social mobility, for example, constitutes one of the major works in that area, while Weber's theory of bureaucratic organization has been empirically tested by Udy (1958; 1959; 1961), Blau (1965; 1966; 1968), and others. In their central propositions, however, Weber and Sorokin remain almost as remote from empirical verification as Spengler (who, of course, would reject the legitimacy of such verification in any case). Sorokin's methodological holism—relating all to all in sociocultural systems that embrace whole civilizations and can be comprehended only in their entirety—ensures that his theory will never be adequately tested against empirical data. And while Weber's insights, grounded in historical research, seem to explain that history, few of his predictions are of a sufficiently specific nature to permit their testing against developments since Weber's time.

The rise and fall theorists, like the other groups of theorists we have considered, offer explanations of societal change which, although in part "convincing," remain untestable. To the extent that theories of societal change re-

[14] Ogburn's use of "culture" embraces both the social and the cultural: his "material culture" corresponds roughly to technology, while "nonmaterial culture" corresponds to all else that is cultural as well as that which is strictly social. Weber traces the development of rationality in economic organization, as well as in numerous areas of culture strictly defined.

main general theories, apparently they will be neither proved nor disproved. Perhaps we can agree with Parsons' pessimistic prediction that when a theory of structural change is available, "the millenium for social science will have arrived. This will not come in our time, and most probably never" (Parsons, 1951: 534).

REFERENCES

Blau, Peter M.
  1965 "The comparative study of organizations." Indus-
        trial and Labor Relations Review 28: 323–38.
  1966 "The structure of small bureaucracies." American
        Sociological Review 31: 171–91.
  1968 "The hierarchy of authority in organizations."
        American Journal of Sociology 73: 453–67.
Dahrendorf, Ralf.
  1959 Class and Class Conflict in Industrial Society.
        Stanford, Calif.: Stanford University Press.
Etzioni, Amitai, and Eva Etzioni, eds.
  1964 Social Change. New York: Basic Books.
Feldman, Arnold S., and Christopher Hurn.
  1966 "The experience of modernization." Sociometry 29
        (December) : 378–95.
Hagen, Everett E.
  1962 On the Theory of Social Change. Homewood, Ill.:
        Dorsey.
Homans, George C.
  1950 The Human Group. New York: Harcourt, Brace
        & World.
Mayhew, Leon H.
  1968 "Society." In International Encyclopedia of the
        Social Sciences. Vol. 14: 577–586. New York:
        Macmillan; Free Press.
McClelland, David C.
  1961 The Achieving Society. New York: Free Press.
Moore, Wilbert E.
  1963 Social Change. Englewood Cliffs, N.J.: Prentice-
        Hall.
  1968 "Social change." In International Encyclopedia of

the Social Sciences. Vol. 14: 365–375. New York: Macmillan; Free Press.

Ogburn, William F.
1922   Social Change with Respect to Culture and Original Nature. New York: B. W. Heubsch.

Parsons, Talcott.
1951   The Social System. New York: Free Press.
1954   Essays in Sociological Theory. New York: Free Press.
1960   Structure and Process in Modern Society. New York: Free Press.
1966   Societies: Evolutionary and Comparative Perspectives. Englewood Cliffs, N.J.: Prentice-Hall.

Parsons, Talcott, and Neil J. Smelser.
1965   Economy and Society. New York: Free Press.

Smelser, Neil J.
1967   Sociology: An Introduction. New York: Wiley.

Sorokin, Pitirim A.
1947   Society, Culture, and Personality. New York: Harper.
1959   Social and Cultural Mobility. New York: Free Press.

Udy, Stanley H.
1958   "Bureaucratic elements in organizations." American Sociological Review 23: 415–18.
1959   " 'Bureaucracy' and 'rationality' in Weber's organization Theory." American Sociological Review 24: 791–95.
1961   "Technical and institutional factors in production organizations." AJS 67: 247–61.

Weber, Max.
1964   The Theory of Social and Economic Organization. New York: Free Press.

White, Leslie.
1949   The Science of Culture. New York: Grove Press.

Index

A

D

E

F

Family, 23, 24, 28, 35, 38, 41, 42, 44, 45, 45n–46n,
    47–49, 50n, 54, 55, 87
Fertility, 67
Folk-urban continuum, 44, 45, 121, 124
Functionalism, 33, 39, 54–56, 63, 67, 69, 70, 94,
    118–123, 128n, 135
    See also Theories, equilibrium, systems
Functions, 21, 22, 31, 32, 70, 129, 130

G

Gemeinschaft, 10n, 27–30, 112
General evolution theory, defined, 57
    See also Theories, evolutionary
Gesellschaft, 10n, 27–30
Goal attainment, 39, 54–56, 69n, 69–71, 72n
Government authority, 21, 22, 31, 38, 40, 40n, 42,
    49, 52, 54, 55, 86, 89
Great Being, 22

H

Heterogeneity, social, 30–32, 44, 45
Hierarchy, 70
Holistic interrelations method, 102, 103, 135, 136

L

Labor, 46, 47, 85, 92, 114
Latent pattern maintenance. *See* AGIL
Law, 23–25, 33, 46
Legitimacy, 104–110, 125, 136
  See also Authority

M

Markets, 41, 42, 44–47, 49, 52, 114
Migration, 67
Mobility, social, 38, 42, 46, 47, 136
Mobilization, 46, 49
Modernization
  defined, 36–39
  economic, defined, 52–53
  See also Theories, evolutionary, modernization
Money, 41, 42, 46
Monopoly capitalism, 90, 93
Moral density, 34, 45, 47, 129
Mortality, 67
Music, development, 113, 114
Mutation, 16, 16n, 30, 129

N

Nationalism, 46
Natural selection, 16, 129

U

Urban life, 28, 29, 45n–46n
Urbanization, 37, 41

V

Values, 71, 118, 132, 134n

W

Wesenwille, 27